Uwe Wieckenberg (Ed.)

Founders
of Eritrea's Education System

Educational Biographies

Bildungstransfer Verlag

Die Deutsche Nationalbibliothek verzeichnet diese Publikation in der Deutschen Nationalbibliografie; detaillierte bibliografische Daten sind im Internet über <http://dnb.d-nb.de> abrufbar.

2. Auflage/second edition 2015

Herausgeber/editor:
Uwe Wieckenberg, Bildungstransfer GmbH, Heidelberg
Verlag/Publisher: Bildungstransfer Verlag, Heidelberg
Redaktionelle Bearbeitung/Editing: P. Hailemariam, K. Müller, M. Spengler, U. Wieckenberg
Umschlaggestaltung/Layout: Bildungstransfer GmbH, Heidelberg
Herstellung/Production: Books on Demand GmbH, Norderstedt

Die Veröffentlichung der ersten Auflage dieses Buches wurde unterstützt von der GFA Consulting Group Hamburg. The publication of the first edition of this book was supported by GFA Consulting Group Hamburg.

ISBN: 978-3-941972-03-2

Contents

Acknowledgements

As is so often the case, this book could not be published without the suppport of many. First of all, I'd like to thank our thirteen „special cases" (I hope they now can smile about this term) who did a great job during their distance studies and who had a heavier workload than others because of the additional aptitude test they had to pass. During this project I gained a deep insight into exceptional biographies under extraordinary circumstances. These biographies are outstanding examples for humans who have acquired knowledge and experience much more outside of educational institutions than inside (and still do).

I also extend my deep gratitude to the other consortium partners Prof. Dr. Rolf Arnold (University of Kaiserslautern), Peter Gerstlauer and Andreas Meyn (GFA Consulting Group Hamburg) and Tesfamariam Tekie (ECOSOC Asmara). Complex projects like this can only be handled and carried out successfully when different people with different competences work as one unit. Furthermore, GFA Consulting Group kindly supported the publication of the first edition of this book.

Special thanks are due to Petros Hailemariam, director general of the research and human resource department in the ministry of education, Asmara. His serenity, connected with a great deal of experience in many fields reflected in his texts as well as in many conversations, left a lasting impression.

Uwe Wieckenberg

Preface

This book documents 13 Eritrean education biographies, created during the post gradual distance study programme "School Management" conducted by the Technical University Kaiserslautern.

All authors are leading members of the Ministry of Education in Eritrea. They actively have participated in freeing the country located in the eastern part of the African Continent and have simultaneously built up the co-educational and educational system under most difficult circumstances.

A consistently notable contingency was found in all biographic self-reflections, which had decisively influenced the authors and actors curriculums: The three decenniums long fight for Eritrea's independence, the formation of an educational system, and simultaneously the active design of their own education biography.

The imponderableness of fighting for freedom made it impossible to plan professional careers. Most of the time, the academic education had to be discontinued and it was all but certain, if and when it could be resumed.

The biographic approach of educational science was orientated on the understanding of biography as mirror of manifold experiences of a lifelong process that influenced the personal development and actions of individuals. Studying the Eritrean educational biographies made quickly aware that for certain social situations, informal and improvised studying was of high significance.

Rolf Arnold[1] understands pedagogic as life forming and at the same time altering science. It is about defining and creative forces of education. According to that understanding, documentary biographies are exemplarily for Eritrea's "Nation Building Process".

According to Jochen Kade[2], a German education scientist, a biography is always the result of individual perception and acts of interpretation. In that respect, it is the told story of life. The concept of biography places the individuality and subjectivity of the addressee's pedagogic actions into the focus point. He shall be seen as a whole person and not as an abstract conglomeration of sociologic characteristics.

From this point of view, this book will not contribute another research result but trigger more interest on educational science for biographic research.

Uwe Wieckenberg
Heidelberg/Germany, June 2015

---

[1] Arnold, Rolf: Selbstbildung – oder: Wer kann ich werden und wenn ja wie? Hohengehren 2010.

[2] Kade, Jochen: Erziehungswissenschaftliche Bildungsforschung im Spannungsfeld von Biographie, Karriere und Lebenslauf". In: bildungsforschung, Jahrgang 2, Ausgabe 2, 2005.

Context of the Educational Biographies

By Uwe Wieckenberg

This book is one of the outcomes of the project "Post- and Undergraduate Studies for the Ministry of Education, Eritrea" funded by the European Union. The project took two and a half years and started in January 2009 with three German consortium partners, the University of Kaiserslautern, the GFA Consulting Group Hamburg and the Institut fuer Bildungstransfer, Landau.

The other – more important – outcomes pertain to 47 Master certificates, 10 first degree equivalent and 111 diploma level equivalent certificates.

The Master programme has been developed for employees of the Ministry of Education Eritrea and is based on the accredited Distance Study Programme "School Management" at the Technical University of Kaiserslautern.

This programme was composed of two parts: basic studies and specialized studies. The basic studies consisted of different subjects in the broad field of School Management which includes relevant topics and subjects in various fields of the personal, institutional and systemical level of the educational system. Examples are

- Pedagogy and School Development
- Assisted Learning: From Teaching to Counselling of Learners
- Change of Learning Culture
- Pedagogical Leadership
- Change Management and Organisational Development
- Criteria for Assessing the Quality of Teaching

- Development of Teaching and Learning Processes
- Team Building and Communication
- Emotional Competence as a Core Competence of School Leadership
- Human Resource Development and Human Resource Management
- School development as a tool of system development
- Quality Control and Quality Management
- External Evaluation and School Inspection
- Research Methods in Social Sciences for School Evaluation.

In the "specialized studies", starting in the third semester, the learners could choose among several specializations, such as "Curriculum Studies", "Educational Planning & Administration" and "Educational Supervision/Accreditation".

In addition to the study texts the programme consisted of face-to-face tutoring seminars and workshops. The learners had to submit several assignments, such as term papers, seminar papers, portfolio, and they had to pass written examinations. All in all a huge workload during the four semesters and a great challenge for the self-motivation: distance learning means learning alone with the help of learning materials and study texts at a distance from one's teacher or lecturer. The learners are separated from their lecturers in space and time but they are still being guided by them.

One of the biggest advantage of distance learning is the fact that learners are able to learn and study beside their job. They have the flexibility or the freedom of choice when and where they study – of course within a given timeframe. Furthermore learners are guided through a support structure that enables them to access those who are available for consultation and support: the tutors, the administrative staff and even lecturers by sending them an e-mail.

The feeling of distance is very often not caused by geographical distance but by the lack of accessibility to needed information. During this programme we tried hard not to make the learners feel the distance. But – on the other hand – they have to feel responsible for their own learning path and continuous motivation.

This study programme had one particular feature: although it is a post-graduate course, which means that students are required to proof that they have a first academic degree, 13 learners – leading members of the Ministry of Education – were not able to present the necessary academic credentials for several reasons, for instance because the documents had been lost during the struggle for independence.

For cases like this, the University of Kaiserslautern provides a unique opportunity to compensate the missing credentials: the aptitude test. This is a sign that general education and the world of work are slowly coming closer. The magic words are "recognition of prior learning". Candidates who do not have the requested credentials can compensate them by having a minimum of five years of relevant experience in the respective professional field. In addition, they have to work out a detailed portfolio which is composed of documents proofing the sound professional experience containing in particular

- a letter of motivation which shows the candidate's development of his own competencies
- a curriculum vitae
- school report cards (if available)
- certificates of examinations in continuing training.

The aptitude test concludes with an oral examination in which candidates must prove a deeper knowledge, own experiences and competencies in the following areas:

- planning and design of didactical concepts for schooling in complex contexts

- realisation of innovations in school development and change of learning culture
- counselling and supporting of teachers
- management of educational institutions
- topics and models of education policy
- quality assurance and evaluation.

The 13 texts of this book derive from the letters of motivation, in which the learners present their personal reflections about their educational and professional biography.

Abbreviations

ELF	Eritrean Liberation Front
EPLF	Eritrean Peoples' Liberation Front
ESECE	Eritrean Secondary Education Certificate Examination.
IIEP	International Institute for Educational Planning, Paris, France
MoE	Ministry of Education
NGO	Non Governmental Organisation
UNESCO	United Nations Educational, Scientific and Cultural Organisation
UNICEF	United Nations International Children's Emergency Fund
TVET	Technical Vocational Education and Training
VET	Vocational Education Training

I. Teaching in Unsettled Times

A Soldier Hits the Books Again

By Ghirmai Estifanos

Above all I would like to say "thank you" to the Technical University of Kaiserslautern for the commitment to support the staff of the Ministry of Education Eritrea to enhance their competencies by providing different qualifications through distance studies.

David Pratt 1994, in his book curriculum planning said:

"We live in an age of promise and an age of peril. While some of the international tensions of the cold war have relaxed, enough nuclear and chemical weapons remain stockpiled to destroy civilization. In many countries, more political prisoners are jailed and tortured and thousands continue to die in conflicts. Agriculture has never been more efficient or productive, but millions of adults and children around the world are starving. This is the world that education and training inhabits, the world that education and training, in general, and curriculum, in particular must address. In this world it is the role of education to enhance human well-being by promoting learning".

I am an Eritrean working in the Ministry of Education at the Department of Technical and Vocational Education and Training. After the completion of my secondary school education I studied two years advanced diploma course at Bahar-Dar Polytechnic Institute Ethiopia and graduated in metal technology. After my graduation I was recruited as a teacher in the Ministry of Education Ethiopia and worked as a machine shop instructor at Bahar-Dar Polytechnic Institute.

In the summer of 1977 I joined the Eritrean Peoples Liberation Front and served as a combatant and at the maintenance and repair of the artillery section. I also served as a teacher in the liberated areas with in the stronghold of the Eritrean Peoples Liberation Front.

After liberation I was assigned as a machine shop instructor in Asmara Technical School. From there I went to Taiwan to study precision machinery for four months. After my return I was placed as a director of Maihabar Technical School until 2001. When I was working as a director at this school I was sent to Germany for four months to study the management of training institutions. I also participated in other short courses in Mauritius, Japan and China. In 2001-2002 I studied at the University of Huddersfield UK and awarded a Bachelor of Education in Technical and Vocational Education. Since 2003 I am working, first as a unit head and then as a director of the curriculum planning and development division at the TVET department Ministry of Education.

The issue of my motivation to study in the master programme of school management is that the government of Eritrea is currently undertaking a transformation of the whole education System and this is supported through funding from external partners. Thus my responsibilities are to work for the success of these projects through the development of an up-to-date policy as well as programmes and guidelines for vocational education and training with the appropriate management skills and good governance for the benefit of the use and the society at large.

The intensified situation of global competition and high numbers of low skilled workers in the workforce are some of the challenges every nation faces. Structured action in the public sector of education and training could help to prepare individuals for today's society and is vital for future competitiveness and innovation.

Vocational Education and Training (VET) plays a key role in this picture by providing the skills, knowledge and competences needed in the labour market. It is therefore an essential part of any Education and Training system.

Technical and Vocational Education and Training is one of the sub-sectors of education which could play a big role in revitalising the devastated economy of Eritrea by supplying trained personnel of various levels and types of skill, thus creating better employment opportunities for those achieving vocational qualifications. Realizing the significance of the sub-sector for poverty alleviation and national development, the government of Eritrea is putting huge investments in education and training.

Although a lot of progress has been made in drafting educational policy papers in general and the management of vocational education and training programmes in particular, including hiring international consultants, vocational education and training delivery requires continuous developmental effort as the society itself is changing at a faster rate, because of technological, economic and social development. Thus vocational education and training system is increasingly expected to be responsive to the changing demands.

The international expertise is very crucial for developing countries, as we do not have to reinvent the wheel. Anyway, if the educational leaders, researchers, and practitioners like me are not prepared to approach such issues and challenges of the education system in the appropriate way due to limited competency, any effort made will not bring any change to the country's economy and the society's well being. The report of the World Bank research results published in July 2008 says that better living conditions are a consequence of better governance and not vice versa.

As explained by Prof. Dr. Hans-Gunter Rolff (School Development: Instruments and methods, study text 6.1), "the centre point of school development is the improvement of the quality of teaching and learning through teachers, parents and students". Thus, any reform towards that end will not do any good to a society unless there is good governance and efficient and effective management skills in planning, organising, controlling and directing. These are the bottlenecks or needs I perceive for improvements within the sphere of my responsibility.

Hence I do believe that the programme of school management offered by the University of Kaiserslautern is designed to foster the development of such personnel and prepares them to approach such issues from multiple perspectives. Thus by studying in the Master's Programme of School Management at the University of Kaiserslautern through distance learning, I will be able to shoulder my responsibilities effectively and efficiently.

I will keep on working on vocational education and training policy development based on the international experience that matches the cultural, social and economic context of my country and on implementing quality training with good governance, so that the youth in particular and the society at large will have a bright future and good livelihood.

Discipline and Handwork are the Key to Meet Expectations

By Kaleab Andemicael

Different writers and philosophers defined learning as a process to permanent changes of behaviour as a result of experience, a process that brings together cognitive, emotional and environmental influences and experiences for making changes in one's knowledge, skills and values. I agree in both descriptions.

It is true that one is said to be learning, if he/she has made permanent change in the way she/he is thinking, acting and doing things. These behavioural changes in knowledge, skills and experiences come through proper guidance and instruction (teaching). Instruction plays a great role in shaping our learning styles. Learning and instruction (teaching) are two faces of the same coin. They are interdependent on one another; one can learn while he/she is teaching. In addition we learn through goal oriented as well as planned instruction.

The other way we can learn is incidental learning, (without full awareness of it) and informal learning that is through co-operation and participation in different human activities. We learn formally or informally, through interaction with society as well as from our experiences.

Experience is a school from which people might be learn a lot. We always learn through our daily activities of our social life, although we are not aware of it. I believe that some people lack the habit and the experience to document their daily activities. I personally lack the habit and practice of keeping my portfolios up to date. A Portfolio is an organised diary of activities of people's work.

Most people do a lot, but document very few or sometimes none of what they have done. I have done a lot of activities and have experiences as a farmer how to plough and do the other activities of a farmer, as a student, as a teacher through the three different levels and as a curriculum developer. But because of the lack of experience of documentation, lengths of time, changes of working areas in different regions, availability of space and luck of proper technology, I am not able to present all of my valid documents. However, I can say some thing about some of them.

I do not have much to say about my experience as an elementary school student. I want to say something about my student life in Saint George secondary and middle school 40 years ago. Saint George is a secondary school which is found in Mendefera, capital city of the Seraye province at that time, but now Zoba Debub. It was one of the popular high schools in Eritrea at that time. Its teachers were natives, Indians as well as some from Ceylon.

I am a descendent of a farmer's family. My village is about 40 km from the high school. While I was in the elementary school, I was living with my family, learning as well as helping them in the farm lands and watching after animals. However, I was not a weak student, as I had an ambition to become a teacher which was the most liked and respected job at that time. At the end of grade 6 when I passed to grade7, I came to a new environment, experienced city life and a big school with almost 1000 students. I had to live with a group of five friends renting a small room and we prepared our own food, cooking and baking bread ourselves. As we were looking to a bright future, we were very cooperative as well as programmed students. When one is preparing food another brings a bundle of wood for making fire from the surrounding areas, while the others set different questions for a group discussion. We had no beds, we were sleeping on the ground having a carpet as a bed sheet; we had to use the street light for studying. Though the living conditions seemed to be bitter, we were very happy and did not mind it very much. The economic and social conditions were not as severe as today. However, the living standard was very low. Students had to walk for at least five kilometres to get to an elementary school, from 10 to 20 kilometres to get to a middle school for those that were available.

To attend a high school one had to take a national exam of grade 8 and get a minimum of 50. So I took the national exam of grade 8 and passed to grade 9.

The average number of students in the class was 55 to 60. The majority of students were above 18 years old and were coming from the surrounding rural areas as well as from remote villages. The students were working hard and there was high competition among each of us for prizes. Our method of study was memorization, one recited while the other looked whether he skipped or not. We had study groups consisting of two or three people most of the time male students. At that time it was not very common to have a study group that included female students because of cultural/traditional inhibitions. Every one was good enough in solving mathematical problems. In subjects such as mathematics, physics and chemistry we were working and helping each other, while for subjects such as history, geography and biology, we were studying independently depending on memorization. I can say that the study groups we had at that time shaped our future life and inclinations. I really wonder why the mathematical ability and skill of our students is now declining.

Teachers' methods of teaching were mostly dominated by lecture method, but sometimes demonstration method was also used in the case of science. However, no group work or project work were given. Teaching methods lacked the cognitive strategies that act directly on the object of learning; such as repetition, organisation and elaboration. The teaching methodology was merely teacher dominated and not participatory, at least within the majority of the teachers at that time.

However, I shouldn't pass without mentioning some of the best teachers and the teachers used teaching aid materials. Some science teachers used laboratories for demonstrations, maps and globes were commonly used by some geography and history teachers. Having said this, students' participation in the preparation of supporting materials was still not very common as this aids were ready made or available from the school. Therefore, I am safe to say that the teaching approach was teacher centred.

The system of assessment was not continuous. It was only based on two exam results: 40% mid and 60% final exam. I can say it was like a trap. Passing mark from grade to grade depended on the grade level and varied from an average of 55% - 60%. The types of questions were not covering all the different domains of knowledge and they did not even take into account the different abilities of groups in the class for some subjects. The same was true for the other subjects except for geography.

After the completion of grade 10, I was selected to train as an elementary school teacher of courses based on my interest. I went to the Jima T.T.I., which is very far away from my area, for two years training. It was new experience with new environment, new people with different languages and different cultures and norms or customs.

The T.T.I was a place where students trained in the teaching profession and teaching ethics. In the institute we learned:

- How to live with people of different languages and cultures in harmony
- Cooperation and sharing of information
- Responsibility to fulfil common goals
- Tolerance in group discussion
- Group work as well as team working.

To fulfil the above mentioned responsibilities in addition to the discussion groups in the class rooms, we had groups organised in blocks of bed rooms having 20 students with everyone having specific tasks such as: leader of discipline of the block of bedrooms, leader for the neatness of the block, leader of organizing tales and jokes in different cultures, leader for organizing picnic and organising funds for the picnic etc.

All the above actives were conducted during spare time outside the instructional time, mostly in the week ends. I was responsible for discipline and neatness of our block, especially for the discipline of the bedroom. Everyone had respect for the others, and should live in harmony among the groups; everyone should be around his bed by the time 10:45 p.m. Neatness of bed room: every Sunday our bed room hall had to be washed with clean water, every student had to set and arrange his bed sheet in a new style made by the committee of designers like a wedding sermon.

The management of the institute's neatness committee evaluated every hall every Sunday morning and ranked the performances accordingly as 1, 2 and 3. The reward for the 20 students was going to a picnic to some areas outside the town at the expense of the institute. Our hall had two chances in both semesters. One a picnic to a place called Bonga, a place of different spices and a market place of coffee; the other picnic was going to the historical place of Abajifar. It was an enjoyable and educational picnic and we learned a lot from it about some of the feudal systems of Ethiopia.

Another experience that I learned from the T.T.I. was the teaching learning approaches from the pedagogically experienced teachers. I learned different methods of presenting a lesson, the way a teacher should treat and handle his/her students and how he/she should cooperate with students' parents and the community as a whole to meet the goal. When I try to reflect on the methodology the teachers were using at that time now, it was "interactive teaching learning approaches" as we call it today. But today everyone is talking about the interactive teaching learning approach as if it was a new finding.

Teachers were giving us assignments and project works in groups. Each group was presenting its finding or idea to the class and answered questions raised by the class.

Another regulation of the institute was that every student had to participate in at least one club (curricular activity) to gain knowledge beyond the teaching learning methodology. In this case I had two clubs the agriculture club and the art club.

The main goal of the institute was to produce both academically and professionally competent elementary school teachers. Every student had to fulfil and satisfy the standards of the school. So I was performing all my duties based on schedule and my academic performance was very good

In the institute I learned and developed a habit of working according to the following schedule: time for enjoyment, time for reading and upgrading my knowledge, time for helping and visiting friends and relatives.

All the above habits that I developed in the institute helped and shaped me in my career when I was assigned as an elementary school teacher. I graduated with the qualification of 10+2 diploma as an elementary school teacher.

I was first trained as an elementary school teacher in 1974. When I was assigned in a small elementary school as a teacher, I was teaching all subjects: Amharic, mathematics, social studies and science. I had daily attendance sheet of students as well as a mark list of each subject. Because of my activities, I was recommended to train as a mathematics middle school teacher through a crash programme in the Addis Ababa College of Education. After the training I was assigned as a mathematics teacher in a middle school and a high school.

My activities enabled me to be rewarded as best school teacher of the region and I received a merit entitled "Misgun Memhir" means a good teacher with some incentives. Some of the selection criteria for "Misgun Memhir" were to know the respective subject matter well, to contribute something to the school, to teach with supportive teaching aid materials, to be punctual, to support students in extra time and to cooperate with colleagues and the community.

When I was a secondary student I had a dream of becoming a good mathematics teacher, influenced by one of my best mathematics teachers of grade 10 at that time. To actualise my vision I took the Ethiopian Grade 12 National Examination for Entrance to the university and I scored a very good mark.

However, because of a personal problem I was not able to continue my education as a regular student. So I chose another path, to continue through on the job training, through summer programmes (kiremts). The duration of one "kiremt" is almost three months.

Rewards and incentives motivated me to work hard, build my capacity and upgrade myself through short and long programmes of training. So I was able to build my capacity and upgrade my qualification from certificate level to diploma level and then to the degree level. I can say I was a student as well as a teacher for the last 30 years.

After I got my diploma the Ministry of Education gave me an internal scholarship to continue my education as a regular day student in the University of Asmara and I attended it in the academic years of 2000 to 2002 and got my Bachelor degree.

I served and taught as an elementary school teacher and elementary school director, middle school and high school mathematics teacher for 33 years. After my first degree, I was shifted to my current work place in the Department of General Education Curriculum Division as mathematics curriculum developer (DGECD). Here I learned a lot with my colleagues and through my personal efforts about text book writing and the use of technology such as the use of the computer.

In my current department we revised the scope, sequence and the syllabus guides of the new mathematics curriculum for the three levels: elementary, middle and high school levels. We also prepared textbooks for the elementary and middle school levels under the guidance of the Curriculum Division through different phases. The panel members were two, but now we are three and we work as a group. I can even say we have become a team. We conduct hot academic discussions among us.

We divided our work in different phases as follows:

a) First phase: We prepared text books and teacher's guides' for grades one and six as well as a workbook for grade one.

b) Second phase: We prepared mathematics textbooks and teachers' guides' for grade three and seven and piloted for two years. From the feedback gathered from teachers, students and parents we incorporated the necessary feedback. Then after the approval of the quality control committee in the DGE the books got published.

c) Third: through the same process we published textbooks and teachers' guides' of grades 4, 5 and 8.

d) Now, we are in the final stage of writing grades' 9-12 mathematics textbooks' and teachers' guide in collaboration with Asmara University mathematics staff members.

I had a dream when I was a student. My first dream was to become an efficient effective mathematics high school teacher. When this dream was fulfilled another dream arose, that is to get a second degree. But this dream is not yet fulfilled; I am striving to do so. Human beings are never satisfied.

All the ways I have come through were not straight and have many ups and downs. I tried to upgrade my academic performance and my professional skills through different means. When I try to see things and evaluate all the ways I have come through and the experiences I gained and developed after taking this important course for the Masters degree through the distance program education of the University of Kaiserslautern in Germany, I really admire and thank the different professors preparing these very important different modules with important related topics to my current profession and contextual field to my country. The courses I have taken up to now have helped me a lot to see things through different angles and prospective.

Education is a Life Long Process

By Mehreteab Dirar Gebresilassie

Education is a life long process. Some writers express the necessity of education in one's own life saying that education starts in the womb and ends in the tomb.

I was, I am and I will be motivated to learn as long as my mind and body are healthy. Age is not a barrier to learning. In fact, as we grow maturity of learning and thinking go parallel and a person's knowledge and ability go parallel provided the prerequisite favour the concerned individual.

When I was enrolled in Kaiserslautern University I felt quite satisfied for gaining the opportunity and till now I did my assignments and read all the study texts. I had already profited a lot from the distance education materials in developing my competences in the field of education.

For example, if I take Module 3 "Teaching Quality" I came to know a lot about what "Good Teaching" is. I have been acquainted with some of the criteria of good teaching derived from experience. From this I knew the basics of the variety of methods by means of which teaching quality is measured and how it can be increased. Above all I gained an opportunity to introduce myself with the dynamic latest philosophy of education and its pedagogy. This module provided me with basic concepts and practices of teaching and evaluation of teaching quality. From this my gains are procedures connected with international studies, their aims, methodological designs and their main research findings on teaching. This has definitely widened the horizon of my understanding of research findings on educational issues; another important profit that I gained is about the significance of "International Studies" in relation to quality teaching and their categorisation in the context of world wide comparative studies. From this I got a rich storage of knowledge about the classification and inventory of research methods used in the studies. Another yield of the above referred module is about tests, surveys, observation and video studies that were categorised in the context of research works. From this I got the know-how of how to relate the results of the studies with the teaching research and the development of teaching in schools. Another is the significance of the yields of the comparative studies on teaching research and development presented and discussed in terms of their importance for the measurement of teaching quality. This gave me an opportunity to relate the yields of teaching research with the development of teaching in the schools in my own country. From this I am able to realise the exact position of the schools in my home country and have begun to be aware of the way we have to pass through in order to reach the results of the international standards of quality teaching.

The same is also true about the study text dealing with curriculum research and teaching development. From this I gained the most important ideas such as differences and similarities of the curriculum research and about the need and importance of international comparative studies for the development of teaching. Here, I am equipped with the techniques of telling the difference between important terms of scientific methodology in education and teaching development. Another significant gain from this study text is about the essential aspects of learning and instruction relevant for teaching development. This covers learning styles and types of learners and the basic concepts of the methods of instruction relevant for teaching development. From the contents of this portion I have got a store of knowledge to identify the link between teaching development and quality teaching as well as educational standards. Another part of the study text deals with the possibilities for examining teaching in the field and the methods for possible application such as tests, questioning and observation. From this part I got vital knowledge as how to clarify the link between teaching development and professionalism on the one hand and teaching development and the level of self-direction of students on the other hand. This text also deals with the strategies and techniques of teaching development using examples of peer observation, peer teaching and teacher training. From this I got to distinguish essential strategies and methods of teaching development and knowledge about the development of school based curricula methods that inculcate systematic professional group work, a method based on feedback, peer coaching and teacher training.

However, in the middle of the process I was informed that my effort to study was not accepted concerning my education and qualification. This has prickled my motivation to learn. All my secondary level education including teacher training and finally higher education were obtained through a continuing education programme. This was in addition of carrying out my job as a teacher for over forty-four years. I am determined to finish the course successfully if I am allowed to do so.

Above all, it was in the job as a teacher and the satisfaction that I amassed as the result of further education were in reality my maximum happiness and satisfaction. Here I developed competencies in reading, writing, speaking and listening the four language skills in English and the vernacular languages. Besides, I benefited in getting to be literate in all academic areas as well as in arts, natural sciences and social sciences. I could say with certainty that the basis of my education was laid here. In addition I attended many workshops and seminars offered by the Department of General Education in order to increase my competence as curriculum developer. It is impossible for someone to become curriculum developer without one's self-development in education. A curriculum developer needs to possess a variety of competences and that is of course through self-development in education.

I was employed by the Ministry of Education of Ethiopia in 1963 and after independence I am serving my country up to the present. I am not able to show my employment certificate due to

33

plain reasons. However, you can refer to the Ministry of Education of the state of Eritrea. I remained a teacher throughout my service of forty-four years at different levels from elementary up to secondary and at present I am a curriculum developer in the Department of General Education. As curriculum developer I took part in the preparation of teaching materials in the elementary and secondary levels. I took part in considerations how teaching is taking place and the strong and weak features of the text books in a pilot project in 26 elementary schools in Eritrea.

My educational progress was achieved through continuing evening and summer programmes sponsored by the Ministry of Education of Ethiopia before independence from 1967 to 1990 with frequent intervals of time. Here my educational vision was fulfilled to a certain extent giving rise to the development of my educational status to the level of BA in history and I taught the subject for over twenty years in secondary level from grade nine to grade twelve.

In my present position, I have developed enough knowledge and skill in thinking about educational issues in the field of education itself. Thanks to the University of Kaiserslautern in Germany that my outlook in education and school development has deepened and increased in scope and sequence.

My curriculum vitae exposes over 40 years of teaching experience throughout Eritrea in different places and at different times and at different grade levels. I started with teaching with less knowledge and skill than I have today.

Discontinuity As a Constant

By Tesfalidit Tecle Ghebremariam

Writing a letter of motivation reminds me of my entire struggle for edification, so that I am forced to give you a brief account of my schooling and my quest of learning experience.

From 1963 - 1970 I have completed my elementary and junior school successfully. Then I continued my high school education and learned grade nine and ten; however, due to the war exploding in 1973 in Eritrea, all schools were closed and so I was not able to continue my education. Then in 1974, I completed 11th grade and for the second time stopped for 2 years. But, later in 1977 I continued to learn and completed my high school.

Although my intention was to participate in the High School Leaving Certificate Examination and to join university, the situation in my country was not helpful, because the war for independence was intensified. Thus, I withdrew from school and went to join the armed struggle. Since I have joined the struggle until 1983 I did not get any chance to continue my education due to the inconvenience of my assignment.

Fortunately, after some years, I was assigned to work in the department of education both as a teacher and as a school principal in elementary and boarding schools. This created a precious opportunity for me, because I was able to think about continuing my career development in education. Likewise, being a member of staff of the department of education has motivated me to keep on reading and improve myself to cope with the demanding career that I had. As a matter of fact, the teacher training programmes that were organised during the summer helped me to think and upgrade my knowledge and understanding of school management as a concept.

Needless to say, one year after Eritrea got its independence in 1991, I participated in the High School Leaving Certificate Examination. Despite all the hardship of the armed struggle, shortage of reading materials and inconvenient learning atmosphere, through the effort I invested for developing my career, finally I succeeded in the matriculation and joined The University of Asmara in 1993. Although I completed my 1st year study effectively, I could not continue to learn, because I have been assigned again to work in remote part of Eritrea as dean of student affairs. However, the completion of the 1st year in the university has broadened my theoretical knowledge and understanding regarding different aspects of management.

The following year, I was assigned as a school principal in one of the intermediate technical schools in Eritrea. In addition to the work experience that I had, the knowledge that I got through formal learning enabled me much more to run the school, handle problems cautiously and look effects from different perspectives in order to reach solutions. As an intermediate technical school principal I have to deal with different teachers, create a conducive learning atmosphere and make linkage with employers and other stakeholders in order to promote best performances.

Having said this, in 1996 I got a chance to be enrolled as a post graduate student in management in Leicester University through distance education and I successfully obtained my post graduate diploma from that university in 1998. The coverage of the courses included: "The Effective Manager", "Managing in Organisations" and "Managing the Organisation". In addition to the written assignments I have taken two controlled exams and finally I did a comprehensive research on the title "Assessment on Unemployment Problems and Alternative Solutions for Maihabar Technical School Graduates" and submitted my dissertation as a partial fulfilment to my post graduate diploma. This learning opportunity has helped me a lot to have a broader understanding of management and leadership as concepts and to apply the different skills that I have acquired in my studies by adapting them to our state of affairs.

Nevertheless, in order to implement the contemporary management principles, create an encouraging and enabling environment for learners and to improve the learning culture, I have realised that I must own the expertise to demonstrate how to deal with school development that encompasses the teaching and learning process, the personnel and the organisational developments. Hence, I believe that such skills and competencies will be acquired partially through formal learning, and partially through informal learning and work experiences. For that reason, I have always the motivation to continue to learn more.

In light of this, the continuous exposure that I got from different workshops and seminars in educational management encouraged me to go on thinking of more formal learning and to upgrade myself with higher qualification to fulfil necessary professional requirements as expected.

According to my current job, as the head of the supervision unit, I have to organise and lead the supervisory activities in the TVET schools; I have to offer pedagogical support to instructors and provide professional assistance to school principals. Moreover, for the sustainable teaching and learning process, together with the team of supervisors, we monitor and evaluate the quality of education by providing constructive feedback to the schools under supervision.

Attending the Kaiserslautern distance education programme enabled me to understand different educational management issues thoroughly related to the international practice and for that reason provides me in-depth theoretical and practical school based applications. Throughout my learning experience during this course, I could apply many theoretical concepts from the various lessons in the different texts and modules to my current job and this motivated me more to be interested in my study.

Since 1983 up to 1991, I have worked in elementary and boarding schools both as a teacher and as a school principal. Besides my role as a school principal I also used to be involved in teaching because there was shortage of teachers in most of the schools. Fortunately, the teaching experience has helped me a lot to understand the nature of the learning and teaching process thoroughly. Then from 1994 up to 2005 I worked as dean of student affairs and school principal in Maihabar Intermediate Technical School. At that moment the management course from Leicester University was very supportive and helpful in managing this technical and vocational school. Finally since 2006 up to the present time I am working as a unit head of the supervision unit in monitoring and quality assurance division in the Department of TVET.

As head of supervision unit in the division of Monitoring and Quality Assurance the areas of my responsibility demand to undergo various activities, such as: supervising the performance of schools, offering constructive feedback to the school management and teachers, organising and delivering training as well as monitoring and controlling the overall quality of the education delivered. Based on my experience all teachers and school directors need time to refresh their thinking and try out new ideas or teaching methods in a secure environment. In light of this, together with my team, I have organised different projects that are aimed at improving the quality of training provided in our schools through enhancing the capacity of school management and teaching staff.

My thesis will be about the project "Ensuring quality training In TVET schools by enhancing effective school management" which I implemented with 56 school principals, pedagogy heads and department heads from the 6 technical schools in Eritrea.

Generally, quality learning is concerned with acquiring knowledge that assists learners to develop relevant skills which enable them to be useful and productive members of the society. This happens when students take responsibility for their own learning and are partners of their teachers. Moreover, the assurance of quality is guaranteed when assessment is based on transparent, objective and inclusive procedures with the existence of a knowledgeable, committed and participatory leadership. Therefore the project has emphasised this basic rational as a baseline.

Outcome of this project: Even though the outcome requires time to be internalised within the school context, the overall feedback of the evaluation was encouraging. Three months after the training a follow-up school visit has been conducted and consequently, in most of the schools, the following improvements were observed:

- the school leadership supports innovation, challenges malpractice and becomes committed to learning;
- better understanding and healthy communication among staff members and management has been developed;
- internal supervision initiated by the director and the pedagogy head;
- team work encouraged and initiated;
- school development plan has been set.

In addition to the mentioned improvements teachers and school leadership can diagnose the source of a problem through quiet private discussion, can identify things which are within their control and be clear about what they can do to help. Moreover, they can separate personal and professional issues so that they could have smooth collegial communications. To this end, teachers talk freely about their work and discuss solutions not problems so that learning will improve. Thus it can be concluded that although these improvements are gained as a result of so many other factors, however, the project has played a significant role in enhancing the progress within our schools.

Beyond that I have participated in various training programmes, workshops and visits to different countries to enrich my competences through such exposure.

Firstly, the training I had in "Educational Psychology, Pedagogy, Educational Administration and Computer Application" created a sensational encouragement in my post as the head of an intermediate technical school. It enabled me to perceive things from different perspectives and also uplifted my problem solving ability. Moreover, the pedagogic parts of the training have also raised my know-how in conducting evaluation, in performing internal supervision and in the provision of pedagogic support to my teaching staff. Likewise, the training in computer application has given me the necessary basic skills in using computer aided school reports.

Secondly, in the training "Current Trends and Issues in Vocational Education & Training Policy" conducted in Italy participated 16 countries from Africa, Asia, Europe and Caribbean. As my first exposure outside my country it has been one of the greatest opportunities I had to share experience with different educational officers from different countries. The discussions and presentations held in the training included the review of training systems and their performance and identified reform policies; identified major issues and trends that are central to training policy; examined various approaches to managing and financing training systems and factors underpinning these approaches, etc. To this end, having had such kind of exposure has given me an enormous motivation to put it into practice considering the reality of my school. It's after this workshop I came up with analysing the prevailing practices worldwide in developing training policies and assess their applicability to my own country's state of affairs.

Thirdly, my assignment as a supervisor is closely related to monitoring and assuring the quality of training in TVET schools. For this reason, the training in Quality Assurance was much more appropriate and relevant in improving my competence in order to assure the quality of the training provision. Needless to say, I realised supervision apart from checking and inspecting; it is more of giving support through feedback and organise and deliver trainings for teachers and school principals to promote quality teaching and learning.

Fourthly, in addition to my job as a unit head in supervision, I am currently also a team member in establishing a Centre for Accreditation and Evaluation in the Ministry of Education. One of the main responsibilities of the team has been to prepare Eritrean National Qualification Framework. In this regard, different workshops and seminars were conducted by international experts to raise the knowledge and understanding of the basic principles and milestones for the establishment of National Qualifications Framework (NQF). Moreover, a study tour to South Africa, Botswana and Namibia has given me a great deal of opportunity to practically see and understand the current practice on the area. Although the South African Qualifications Authority is much more advanced and complicated in its implementation, however I have learned from it, in which the main objective of establishing NQF remains in monitoring and assuring the quality of delivery of the different qualifications in the different training institutions. Similarly, the Botswana and Namibian Qualification Frameworks besides their resemblance are good examples for establishing the system in my country. This visit has given me more energy and motivation to put into practice the real context of the educational system in Eritrea. Generally, from the workshops and seminars as well as the study tour I can notice my competence enhanced.

Last but not least, the contents in the research methodology training which included educational research methodology, design and structure of research, a guide to research methods in education and data processing & basic statistics has increased my level of understanding in writing a research.

II. Revolution School Managers

Fighter and Teacher

By Abraham Russom Almedom

When I was a student the system of formal education was divided into three parts: Elementary education from grade 1 to 6, Junior high school from grade 7 to 8 and Secondary Education from grade 9 to 12.

In 1962 I enrolled to school at the age of 7 in a village called Mekerka and after completing elementary level I went to Asmara for perusing my studies and there I completed junior and senior high school up to grade 11 in Itegue-Menen Junior High School and Prince Mokennen Senior High School respecttively. When I completed grade 11 I succeeded an entrance examination for joining to Biedemariam Laboratory School in Addis Ababa (it was a one year preparatory pre-university school for senior high school teachers) in 1972 and from here I promoted to the university and continued my studies until second year in the faculty of science at Haile Sellassie 1st University of Addis Ababa. On the other side starting from grade 11 I was very much interested and greatly influenced by the Eritrean armed struggle for independence and eventually I became a member of a clandestine cell of the liberation struggle and there I was greatly involved in different activities. In 1974 I decided to join the liberation struggle and as a result I withdrew from the university after the mid term of my second year to join the Eritrean Peoples' liberation Front (E.P.L.F). But unfortunately when I went back from Addis Ababa to Asmara all possible means of access to the organization were almost closed because it was difficult to trace the whereabouts of the EPLF during that period of time in particular. Therefore thinking to use it as a camouflage I got employed as a teacher in a private junior secondary school in Asmara. After serving one year as a teacher in the school during the transition period, I was able to join the liberation struggle in 1975.

From 1975 to 1977 I was a fighter, a teacher and literacy programme coordinator. During the time of liberation struggle the first three years I was with the army fighting in the forefront against the Ethiopian regime. In addition, I was also engaged first as a teacher and later as one among the coordinators of a literacy programme in the army battalion in which I was a member. The literacy programme was continually going on by the organisation not only among members of the EPLF, but even among children and adults of the society in the liberated areas, in line with the principle of the EPLF to eradicate illiteracy and to promote literate environment. This was a good exposure which opened me a way to work jointly with other colleagues of the same profession and at the same time to read and analyse various academic and politics books which helped me to broaden my perspectives and to build a valuable and practical experience. By the end of 1977 I encountered a serious leg injury in a battle and as a result my right leg was hurt. Due to this reason the organisation redeployed me to teach in a school named the "Revolution School" which was founded in the liberated area of Sahel province, one of the Eritrean provinces situated in the north.

I went to the Revolution School at the beginning of 1978. At that time the school was used to give teacher induction courses for new assigned teachers and I was fortunate to attend an intensive 1 month induction teacher training programme with other colleagues before getting assigned as a teacher. This training was very informative and useful; it helped me to acquaint and update myself with the educational philosophy, curriculum, upbringing and children psychology and pedagogy. This helped me to broaden my professional experience as well as to contextualise my knowledge and skills with the real situation of the school. Following the training I served in the teaching profession teaching different subjects like math, science and political education. In addition, at a later stage in 1979 I worked as a team leader of a group of teachers in the school and was responsible for coordinating the daily activities and administration affairs of the teachers. Generally during my earlier stay of two years in the Revolution School I had gained a lot through a way of hard work and self-discipline, sharing ideas and practices with others, continuous practice of self-development and work performance evaluation, collaborative work and collective decision making as well as through further developing a culture of reading and regularly listening to radio programmes.

These practices were greatly encouraged by the principles and mission statements of the EPLF which include developing among the members:

- common and shared vision towards the realisation of achieving Eritrean independence and social justice
- unified commitment to the goal,
- good communication and collaborative culture of collegiality
- political awareness as well as academic and professional competence
- collective responsibility and decision making process.

In 1980 I was posted to another department called Department of Social Affairs and worked for two years as a teacher as well as a chief curriculum coordinator in the school for the disabled from 1980-1981. The school was an elementary school with a capacity of about four hundred adult students, catering learners from grade 1 up to grade 5. As a curriculum coordinator I was responsible for planning the educational programme, checking the lesson plan, giving support and guidance to teachers and supervising the teaching and learning process. It is clear at that time I did not have sound professional capacity to bear such high responsibility for curriculum coordination. But because there was a strong will and commitment at the time of the liberation struggle everything was possible through dedicated effort, mutual cooperation and continuous trial and practice. Similarly the learning achievement of the students at that time was quite high because the team efforts and commitment of the teaching staff and the students was tremendously high, too. To me this initial experience was very valuable and an important step in my career development during the later stages of my profession.

After two years I was again returned and posted to the Revolution School for a second time and there I got promoted to a school manager of one of the six semi-autonomous boarding schools formed under the umbrella of the Revolution School. The name of the particular boarding school, I had been assigned to, was called 01 and it had minimum of 500 school age children, 21 teachers, and about 60-70 non-teaching staff including children caretakers, nurses and other administrative staff.

As a school manager I bear the responsibility to ensure the proper functioning and continuous development of the school. To achieve this I have taken measures to monitor the students' well-being, academic achievement, behavioural trend and personal health regularly in accordance with the development and annual plan as well as rules and guidelines of the school. This was done through active participation of the teaching and non-teaching staff. There was strong commitment, collaboration, interaction and team work among the staff when implementing various activities. They were always involved with feelings of ownership and accountability because everybody had a shared understanding about the goal. For each activity there was regular monitoring and evaluation done on monthly and semester base. In addition there was another mechanism whereby a meeting of criticism and self-criticism was called by the respective administrative units, teams, or the next level of hierarchy on weekly, bi-weekly, or monthly base. This was a regular forum for identifying and correcting whatever mistakes or shortfall happened during the time interval between the two meetings; either by own initiative of oneself to confess or other members could raise the issue and criticise somebody in a constructive way. In this way criticism and self-criticism was very instrumental for improving one's own strength in relation to work performance, behaviour or attitude and such practice indeed had great impact for the steady progress and development of each individual as well as for the sustainable improvement of the quality and performance of the particular organisation.

My role in the Revolution School was not limited to being a school manager only. In addition I had teaching responsibility with children during the day and at night with adults who attended classes in grade 8. Apart from this during the struggle time I was also a member of mathematics curriculum panel in the department of research, located in the Revolution School. All the years I stayed there until independence of Eritrea in 1991 being involved in the development of syllabus and textbooks of mathematics for all levels up to secondary. This engagement had played a very effective role in the development of my academic and professional knowledge because I had always to read and refer books, discuss and consult with others in order to be able to prepare a textbook. In addition I had to prepare myself in order to participate and contribute to the discussions held by the panel. In other aspects involving myself in teamwork and group discussion, which was often practiced during the struggle period, assisted me to a greater extent to develop different skills in my life. To reflect on one example: in 1979 we set up a team of six people with the intention to develop our understanding and perspectives in the area of politics. Each one of us was used to take a separate topic by the way of reading different books and other publications to present it in our weekly meetings. In the meeting we discussed on each one's paper and everyone participated and gave his comments critically. We were used to learn a lot from the in depth discussion. The team lasted for a period of five months. From this I can say such engagements helped me to develop gradually certain valuable characters such as the ability of presentation, to build my confidence, the ability to listen and respect the opinion of others, etc.

When reflecting back the time I worked for ten years as a school manger of the boarding school, as a teacher, curriculum and textbook developer, I can say it was really a golden opportunity that enabled me to build up my experience, knowledge and skills on various dimensions most often from practical and experimental hands on activities. The key task in the process was self evaluation and self-reflection accompanied by feedback from evaluation by others. In this way mistakes had been used as learning opportunities and successes were used as opportunities to generate more successes; all in all it helped me to enhance my capacity for self development.

During the time of struggle for independence I had taken four pedagogic professional courses which covered wide areas of educational management, curriculum and pedagogy, child psychology, counselling, guidance and supervision. Such courses had been very essential and relevant to our needs and we were making efforts to communicate the new knowledge and skills in the form of orientation and discussion to our teaching staff in order to improve their professional competence.

After independence in 1991 I continued to work in the Ministry of Education at various positions. In 1991 I was promoted and posted as head of provincial education office and with this responsibility I worked from 1991-1996 in Akele-Guzay Province, which was one of the seven provinces of Eritrea at that time. After this the provincial administration was substituted by regional administrative structure and at that time I was posted as head of regional education office from 1996-1997 in Anseba, one of the six regions in Eritrea. Generally, as a provincial or regional education officer, I bear a responsibility to ensure, according the government's policy, the expansion of equitable distribution of schools from KG to secondary with great focus given to the more disadvantaged areas in the region. Therefore, at that time the main responsibility of the educational office was planning, supervision, provision of administrative support, monitoring and evaluation. In addition I had been attending many short and medium term professional courses of education. Therefore, this was an additional opportunity for me to further develop my experience in the field of educational planning and management. In 1993 I attended and successfully completed a six week training course in educational management at the University of Asmara and this had been very relevant and practical to my area of responsibility. Following this, I completed an advanced certificate education programme in the University of Birmingham, UK in 1994. All these helped me to further develop my competence in the area of educational planning and school management.

In 1996 I got an opportunity to participate in the 32nd UNESCO annual training programme in educational planning and administration in Paris and I completed it successfully.

In 1998 I was transferred to the head quarter and posted as a director of curriculum planning and development division of general education. In this division I am in charge of the curriculum planning and development, including writing of textbooks, extending from kindergarten up to secondary education. I have been working in these areas for the last 13 years and I have bean able to acquire substantial experience. In the curriculum planning and development there are three units comprising 25 subject panels, with a total number of 52 experts.

During the past 15 years I got plenty of opportunities to participate in many international and regional conferences, symposiums, meetings and workshops. I have presented a number of papers in such kind of workshops and I learned quite a number of lessons from other experts through interaction and sharing of experiences. All these have been helpful for my personal and professional development in wide areas of educational domain and particularly in relation to curriculum studies, textbook production and use, literacy programmes, life skills and HIV/AID and other learning areas.

Challenges as a Source of Inspiration for Self-development

By Ghebrezghi Dimam Okbaldet

This is brief history of how I started my career. Here, I present the various stages which tested and shaped my professional development. I feel, I have been in the education system for so long, but with a lot of ups and downs. I faced difficult times and bitter experiences, but feel happy for overcoming most of those challenges and coming to a new and better situation. Moreover, the difficult and harsh environments under which I worked are testimony of the challenges teachers and other professionals in education in many developing countries especially in Africa face. I think this is by no means a curse, but a reality and a path the people in these countries must necessarily pass through. This challenge should be overcome in order to have a new and better situation. I am sure and confident that many people in education face challenges and in their efforts to overcome those challenges, they introduce innovations to bring about changes and development.

I was born in the town called Keren which is located in the central part of Eritrea. It is a town where you find most of Eritrea's ethnic groups. It is truly a multi-lingual and multi-cultural town and I am lucky being able to speak three Eritrean languages right from my early childhood. I studied my elementary, junior and senior secondary education in this very place. After finishing my senior secondary education in 1969, I joined "The College of Teacher Education" in Addis Ababa, Ethiopia. This was a two year college of education where I graduated with a diploma in science education qualifying me to teach general science at junior level. After finishing the college training, I was a teacher, teaching under the "National Service Programme" for one year. Then I was first assigned as a regular teacher to teach science at a junior school in eastern Ethiopia in 1974. After that, I was transferred to another senior secondary school after two years, where I taught biology for grades nine and ten. In 1977 I was again transferred to Eritrea while it was still the colony of Ethiopia and was assigned as a secondary school biology teacher and worked in the present 'Red Sea Secondary School' and 'Asmara Comprehensive Secondary School' for two years. My experience as science teacher in Ethiopia was indeed a very difficult one. It was the time when the Emperor was replaced by a military junta in a military coup. Mass arrests targeting teachers and students were the order of the day. Students were terrorized and teachers were members of different feuding parties. Intimidation, mass killings and arrests continued. There was a unstable and insecure situation throughout the years I was there as a teacher. Moreover, class size was very large and the number of sections I taught was more than fifteen. Whenever I meet students in the street, I could not recognise them. I could not remember their names, because they were too many. In such circumstances I was confused, frustrated and started to think whether it was desirable to continue in the teaching profession or not. My experience as a teacher in those years was really not an exciting one. I was sometimes told to quit teaching because some military in uniforms would come to teach politics and other indoctrination issues in between my sessions.

Then I joined the liberation struggle in January 1981. Here, it was completely a new environment and full of challenges. I first took the military and other essential training as a fighter and then was assigned to "Zero School" as it was called by the front. My experience in the Zero School was indeed very varied and cumbersome. I was first assigned as a science teacher in the elementary school, but after a short period of teaching, I joined the curriculum team to develop science text books and accompanying teachers' guides at the elementary level on top of the teaching profession. In developing the curriculum, we had very few and very old sciences text books to refer. The staff assigned to develop the text books were not even formally trained teachers, let alone curriculum developers. It was really a testing time, but we had no choice and we worked hard, had continuous discussions, consultations and were able to achieve our objective of developing science text books for the elementary level. In the course of developing the text books, we developed a strong team spirit. There was a lot of commitment and dedication which turned into strong collegiality. After finishing developing the texts, I was assigned as head of the science panel, where I also worked as science teacher and laboratory attendant. Being laboratory attendant was another challenge for me; I had no past experience in handling and managing science labs. My main lab orientation was related to the subject of biology. There was no lab manual to refer to and no sound knowledge on ensuring safety in labs. The science lab was very small in size and overcrowding by students was another challenge. The lab was also used as a store, because all the chemicals and other staff were locked inside the lab. I learned through hard work and hands on experience in relation to science lab activities. To my surprise, I was successful in carrying out lab activities as well as other simple demonstrations in this very place.

In 1983 and 1984, while I was teaching in the Zero School, literacy campaign was launched by the front and I joined the programme as head of one sub-region, where I experienced myriads of events, of course some were wonderful experiences and shaped my carrier as an educator and a social worker while others were very risky and some times frustrating. We were working in a very insecure situation and places with a lot of advances at one time and retreats at another. The places were frequented by enemy attacks and incursions. Our activities of providing literacy and other basic social services to the local community were therefore at a standstill sometimes. Moreover, we had no regularly prepared teaching learning materials. We used to prepare them from the local environment, for example chalk from special stones and charcoal, blackboards from animal skins etc. In our literacy classes we also had sessions on health and sanitation, environment, harmful traditional practices like FGM (female genital mutilation), the importance of working in cooperation etc. We also introduced recreation activities like sports in the rural communities. It was an immense experience in giving literacy and other services in such an emergency situation. It really changed my thinking, because it was such a challenging, but interesting experience full of risks, but one that nourished my soul, gave me satisfaction and motivated me to do more.

After the two interesting years in the literacy campaign I went back to the Zero School, where I was assigned as senior supervisor in one region of the liberated areas. This part of the country was also disadvantaged, because there were no schools built before the start of the liberation struggle. Awareness raising campaigns were conducted before starting education in this area. After having good understanding of the value of education, the communities, the schools served, were happy and their children participated in good numbers, even the girls who usually stayed at home were soon encouraged by their parents to participate in education. One boarding school was established for children coming from distant places and the very poor. The school organised cultural activities as part of school programmes and the students and the local community liked it very much. During my supervision visits, I joined the students' activities specially the cultural shows by dancing with them, which was fun and confidence building. The students and teachers liked it and I had no problems to communicate with everyone in the school community. I also joined students during lunch time and we ate together which they liked and had a lot of chat on every issue regarding their schooling and overall development of their region. Eritrea was freed while I was working as the supervisor in this very place.

With the independence of my country in May 1991, I was selected as one of the team members who were assigned to give orientations, seminars and workshops on the educational experiences and programmes of the EPLF (Eritrean Peoples Liberation Front) to the teaching staff who were teaching under the Ethiopian education system. The main objective was to create a forum for teachers who were teaching under the Ethiopian system where they could spell out their experiences, challenges and how they would like to continue as teachers in the new situation and in the new country. We were also supposed to give orientation towards the education system of the EPLF, where at the elementary level the various Eritrean languages were used as media of education (instruction). At the end of the seminars and workshops many teachers were motivated and committed themselves to continue in the profession and contribute to the development of education in their country.

When the orientations and seminars were over, I was assigned as education officer of the Barka Region in September 1991. This region is located in the western lowlands of Eritrea. This region was one of the most disadvantaged regions of the new country and due to underdevelopment and long established harmful traditional beliefs and practices the value attached to education was very low. My main task then was to conduct intensive awareness raising campaigns and make the necessary preparations to open schools in various parts of the region. After some successful contacts and consultations with the communities, they agreed on the opening of new schools in various parts of the region to create education opportunities for the children of that region and we were able to start ten new elementary schools at that time with the scarce resources we had. This was a remarkable start for the region. Here, bringing girls to school was a real challenge and many school age girls did not participate. Distance between settlements was long and did not encourage small kids to attend schooling. Poverty caused by recurrent draughts and shortage of drinking water was another challenge against our efforts to open schools in order to address the educational needs of that region. Despite the various challenges, schooling continued in that region and I am always happy and proud of what I contributed at that time even though it could be very little. At present the region is having more schools and is in a much better situation.

In 1993, I was given the opportunity to go abroad and study. With the help of the government of Eritrea and the British Council, I was able to continue my studies at the University of Birmingham, in the United Kingdom where I got my BA in Educational Management in 1994. It was my first time to go abroad to study. At the beginning everything seemed strange, the climate, the culture, the loneliness etc. My English was not at the desired level, I was not computer literate while the university used computerization extensively. Using the library, using references and term paper writing were all challenges that I had to face and overcome. With commitment and hard work I solved all the challenges and finished my studies with good grades. While being in the United Kingdom, I had the opportunity to visit many places and meet many people from the various parts of the world. This helped me to have broader understanding of what it means to live in multi-cultural and multi-lingual societies and situations. After finishing my studies in the UK, I returned back to my country at the end of 1994.

Then in 1995, I was assigned as head of the teacher education section within the Ministry of Education. At that time the first efforts for updating and upgrading teachers through distance learning were started. I had good opportunity of understanding what the teacher education is all about, when the section was trying to develop training materials to be used for the training of teachers through the distance mode. The consultants' and other experienced teachers' inputs were very helpful in developing my capacity to understand the broader field of teacher training, education and development.

In June 1996, I was assigned to the Division of Adult Education as a director (Now the Department of Adult Education and Media). When I came to this division, I was totally new to the various programmes and activities of adult education. I had to consult colleagues and refer to the few documents available then. I also started to read books and publications on the field of adult education with keen interest. I came to know how large and diverse adult education and learning is. Moreover, I got opportunities to attend many national and international seminars, training workshops and participated in many other development projects.

The first project we developed in the adult education was in 1997 and it was related to literacy. It was with the Swedish International Development Agency (SIDA). Such big partnership project was the first of its kind in our adult education programme. The new partnership project was implemented soon without delay and our adult education activities saw considerable progress since then. In 2003, I was promoted to the post of Director General for the Department of Adult Education and Media.

At present, I am working closely with my other colleagues in our ministry, heading various departments and divisions and I am engaged in developing, signing and following up many development projects related to education and training. For example, I participated in developing the "Education Sector Development Programme (ESDP)", The Education Sector Investment Project (ESIP), The EC Support Programme for Education, various other partnership projects with UNICEF, UNFPA etc. Moreover, as active member of the Ministry of Education, I participated in many international and national training programmes, workshops and seminars. I headed many teams and delegations in important meetings and seminars and presented country papers in the area of adult education, especially literacy. Finally, I feel confident now that I have good background knowledge of education and training both through formal and non-formal experience. Working both at formal and non-formal education provision also enriched my background knowledge of complementary nature of these two ways of education provision.

Learning by Doing - A Manager in the Field

By Petros Hailemariam

At a mature age of about sixty, like mine, I think most people would find it rather awkward and difficult to describe their competences, especially if they lacked formal or official credentials. This arises as a number of questions would come up to one's mind: What are competences anyway? Does one enumerate all the capabilities one supposedly possesses, or would it be more reasonable to focus on a few important ones? How would one judge certain of them to be important and others not? Should this importance relate to oneself or to others? For example, the knowledge and experience one has acquired in bringing up one's children, cooking food or handling people and social affairs wisely might be regarded highly by some people, but not so by others.

Notwithstanding all these issues, and taking into consideration the academic bent of this assignment, I would limit myself to what I consider are the main competences of general signifycance that I believe I have acquired over the course of my life. Meanwhile, I would take competence or capability as the practical knowledge and skills to do or to achieve something.

I consider that the basis for my competences is both formal and non-formal education as well as exposure to real–life situations. In terms of formal education, I think that obtaining a scholarship at the end of the primary cycle to the General Wingate Secondary School (which was one of the best secondary schools in Ethiopia at the time) has left a lasting impression on me. This fairly solid academic grounding had enabled me to pass the Ethiopian School Leaving Certificate Examination (Matriculation) with "very great distinction" and to develop fairly high self–esteem, as well as confidence in dealing with academic or intellectual issues.

I joined the University of Addis Ababa (then known as Haile Selassie I University) in 1969, where I studied science, with a major in chemistry and a double minor in physics and mathematics. During my fourth year of studies and before getting a degree, I decided to leave the University and join the Eritrean People's Liberation Front (E.P.L.F.). After spending about a decade and a half as a 'fighter', I obtained another opportunity for formal education in 1996, whereby, along with about a hundred other government officials, I enrolled in a distance learning programme for the MBA run by the Open University in the U.K. I had completed two out of the three years of study in this programme with "satisfactory results", when our studies were unfortunately interrupted due to the outbreak of the border conflict with Ethiopia in 1998 — again, before getting a degree! To this, I may add a few very short courses that I took on various subjects (journalism, using the computer, etc.) over the years.

I dare say that I obtained the greater portion of whatever competences I possess in the non-formal way, mainly through personal reading, coaching or mentoring and active participation and reflection in facing up to various real–life tasks and challenges.

Two things that have had a lasting influence on me were the books I read on my own on philosophy and politics while I attended the University in Addis Ababa. One of these books dealt with the history of Western philosophy, which was quite novel and perturbing to me. What I found most difficult to grasp was ontology, especially Kant's skepticism as he distinguished "things–in–themselves" from "things–for–us". Thus, reading Jostein Gaarder's "Sophie's World" about a year ago, i.e. after about four decades, has turned out to be quite refreshing for me.

I then also got acquainted with politics. In line with the worldwide, progressive, political movement among youth and students in the late 60's and early 70's, a radical trend had prevailed among college and high-school students in Ethiopia. This prompted me to read a variety of books on politics and eventually to become an ardent, young supporter of socialism, on the basis of Marxism–Leninism. I continued to read books and followed this political line in the field, until about two years before the fall of the Berlin Wall, when the E.P.L.F. officially reviewed some of its basic political tenets and policies. As I reflect on this aspect of my life, two main things come to my mind:

That, out of ignorance and simple–mindedness, I had once sincerely debated during my high–school days in support of the American 'intervention' in Vietnam and that our group was declared the winner; and

That, in spite of my background in natural science and my readings in philosophy, I had long maintained a somewhat unwholesome and dogmatic stance in political affairs.

Thus, I often wonder whether there is not much wisdom in what George Orwell had said about socialism. To paraphrase him: It would be queer not to believe in socialism in one's youth; but it would be equally queer to continue to believe in socialism after forty.

I have always been so fortunate as to be assigned to or employed in jobs that required reading and writing and that obliged me to upgrade my knowledge and skills more or less continuously, especially as a decision maker. As a consequence, during the last four decades, I have read a substantial number of books and articles dealing with politics, philosophy, education, journalism, fine arts, management, etc. In journalism, for example, when I was assigned to serve as editor–in–chief of the first, Tigrigna, government newspaper in free Eritrea in 1991, although I had been writing magazine articles for a number of years, I was obliged to read some books and learn the basics of writing a news story and running a newspaper. This type of reading has played such an important role in the development of my humble knowledge and skills as well as in shaping me as an individual that I consider myself to be largely self-taught.

The second aspect has been coaching or mentoring. Although I have hardly ever gone through any formal coaching or mentoring session per se, there were numerous occasions when my supervisors, fellow employees or professionals who were more qualified and experienced than me graciously and tacitly shared their knowledge and insights with me in the form of advice, suggestions and hints. I would normally use such advice and assistance to widen my horizons and the repertoire of my skills. In my early days in journalism, for example, a colleague indicated to me the significance of the 5 Ws and 1 H (who, what, when, where, why and how) in writing a news story.

The third and probably most important way that has enabled me to gain a number of competences has been learning by doing. During the liberation struggle in particular, it was the norm to assign people to various tasks by merely giving them a few instructions and the responsibility for implementing them. This would normally pose itself as a challenge. In meeting such a challenge, I would usually start by discussing the task with my supervisor and a few colleagues, try to identify the main issues, set priorities, draw a rough plan of action and then implement the plan, while adjusting it by correcting mistakes and attending to shortcomings, and finally evaluate it. Apart from the practical knowledge and experience I would gain in the process, I would also pay much attention during evaluation meetings and try to refer to relevant literature whenever this was convenient.

There has also been a related fourth way, namely learning through observation. Travelling fairly, widely, both inside Eritrea and abroad, has broadened my perspectives. Visiting so many schools in Eritrea over the years and observing teachers and lecturers in action has significantly augmented my understanding of educational issues. Similarly the highly gratifying opportunity of educational study tours and seminars I have had in Singapore, U.K., Denmark, Southern Africa, China, etc. has been another important source of inspiration and practical knowledge for me. I believe that my main competences fall under the following four headings: Education, Management, Writing/Journalism, and Political Affairs.

Teaching: My first encounter with a job in education came during my college days when I worked as a part–time, grade-9 chemistry teacher for about two months in a girls' secondary school in Addis Ababa. I soon assumed the same responsibility as I worked for a year in another secondary school in Harar, a south–eastern province of Ethiopia. Thus, I became a teacher without having had any professional training or even any induction.

In line with my biographically acquired notions of teaching and in the belief that the teacher was the determining factor in students' learning, I was very enthusiastic about transferring some knowledge and skills to the students and influencing their behaviour to some extent. No wonder then that my style became highly teacher centered and that I came across quite a few disciplinary problems with some of the students. This has been a good learning experience for me in two respects. On the one hand, through my participation in teaching and other school activities, I came to have a better idea of what it takes to teach and to manage a school properly. On the other hand, I realised that mere enthusiasm and subject knowledge were not enough to ensure effective teaching and student discipline.

School Administration: I happen to be one of the first few people who were assigned in 1975 to establish a Department of Education and the first E.P.L.F.–run school in the field. Almost out of scratch, we managed to establish the Revolution School, and I served as its deputy–director for a short time. I came back to this primary school and served for two years as its director in 1982, under stringent conditions caused by the war which was raging with Ethiopia and the scarcity of resources in the field. By then, it had turned into a huge boarding school with about 4,000 pupils and 900 staff members. This was a big challenge to me, since I neither had any formal training in educational administration nor adequate experience in managing such a massive organisation.

Nevertheless, since this was already a well-functioning school with many people who had already gained much experience in running it, I decided to take this reality as my humble starting point and to learn how to run the school on the basis of the actual situation and experience. With the assistance of my supervisor and the other key people or heads of various departments, I was able to acquire a fairly good idea of the main objectives, tasks, functions, structure, organisational culture, etc. of the school within a relatively short period of time. Heeding the advice of my supervisor, I generally let things run their normal course for about a year, until I felt confident enough to interact more actively in running the school and in introducing improvements. Eventually, I was able to assume greater personal responsibility and to play a more proactive role in managing the school.

Curriculum Design and Development: In 1975, along with some 30 other fighters, mostly young teachers and college students, I embarked on this new task with no reference other than a few old textbooks. On the basis of our personal experience in education and common sense, and through very lengthy discussions, we managed to put together a 'curriculum' that was used when the Revolution School actually started functioning in 1977. I was also obliged to act as head of curriculum development when I returned to the same school in 1982. Fortunately, by this time, an extensive review of the previous curriculum had been undertaken, much valuable experience had been gained, a number of professionals had joined the school and some reference materials had become available.

Here again, I developed my competences mainly through practice. However, this was much enforced through reading and interaction with professionals. Freire's "Pedagogy of the Oppressed" (1970) was an eye opener. A book by the Russian author Anton Semjonowitsch Makarenko on the upbringing of children helped us to treat children more humanely and appropriately. Lectures given by and discussions with educators from abroad (e.g. an Eritrean educator from the U.K. who visited the field in the early '80s) enabled us to have greater understanding of the curriculum (including the hidden curriculum) and to keep abreast with what were then current developments in education (e.g. concepts such as learner–centred pedagogy and de-schooling.) I also came to get a little acquainted with Piaget's ideas. One of the personal contributions I made during this period was a guideline on adult education, which I prepared by referring to some books on andragogy and which served as the main reference for the literacy campaign that was carried out in the liberated areas in the 80s. To date, I have endeavoured to deepen my understanding of educational issues as I work along or engage in discussions with various experts and international consultants.

Teacher Education: I have intermittently been involved in training teachers (mainly as a coordinator) from my days in the field up to the present. In the field, we generally provided short summer courses for most teachers. Nowadays, I oversee the activities of the Asmara Teacher Education Institute and various in–service training programmes. Although my involvement is generally limited to management, I sometimes participate in the professional aspects as well. Some of these are the reviews of curricula and the preparation of various documents, such as the Master Plan for Teacher Education and Development, the Continuing Professional Development of Teachers, Teacher Career Paths, etc. I have recently served as the focal person in the Ministry for fairly sizeable in–service training programmes, such as the Open and Distance Learning Programme for Upgrading Middle School Teachers to the diploma level (ca. 1,300 participants) and the current Post– and Undergraduate Studies which extend from the Master's to the Diploma levels (ca. 400 participants).

Research: Although my main role in research at the Ministry of Education (MoE) is coordination, I also often get involved in the assessment and editing of research papers. Moreover, I sometimes participate in concrete research activities, such as the extensive study which was conducted about two years ago through the leadership of highly-qualified Eritrean professionals to investigate the causes of the low learning achievement of secondary school students in Eritrea. I had also participated as a researcher in studies concerning Eritrean cultural traditions, the transliteration of Eritrean languages, etc. Indeed, I have been fortunate enough to have an article of mine entitled "The Challenges of Educational Reconstruction and Transformation in Eritrea" published in a book (Mebrahtu, T., Crossley, M., Johnson, D. (Ed.) 2000: Globilization, Educational Transformation and Societies in Transition. Oxford) and to defend our policy of mother-tongue education in an international conference held at the University of Bristol, UK, in 1998. Meanwhile I have maintained a keen interest in educational research findings, especially comparative studies, mainly by reading synopses or short reports on them.

Management: I would basically describe myself as an administrator or a manager. Whatever competences I have in this area had largely been acquired through experience until I obtained the opportunity to study management properly through the Open University's MBA programme in 1996.

To illustrate the range of managerial responsibilities I have assumed over the years, I could mention the following:

In education, I have served as a school principal, an organiser of teacher-training courses, a director-general of research and human resource development, a deputy–head of education under the E.P.L.F. in the field, a coordinator of a literacy campaign in the areas 'behind the enemy lines', the focal person in MoE for appraising, planning and managing the Education Sector Development Programme (2005-09) and its components, an administrator of numerous projects, and a coordinator of various national and local conferences and workshops.

I have also served as a newspaper editor and a director–general of the Print Media and News Agency in the Ministry of Information, as well as a team leader and a committee leader under various circumstances.

Journalism: Here again, I would say that I have developed my competences mainly through practice, although this has often been supplemented by reading. Over the years, I was involved in writing various (mainly political) magazine and newspaper articles. I have contributed to the preparation of textbooks, as well as educational guidelines and policy papers. I also believe that I have acquired a fair degree of competence in editing, both in Tigrigna and English.

Political Affairs: I have been fully involved in the protracted struggle of the Eritrean people for liberation (including the armed struggle) and in the ongoing task of nation building. In brief, I could say that I have participated in almost all aspects of political life in Eritrea, including teaching, awareness raising, organising and policy formulation. The main sources of my competences in this field have been actual practice, individual reading and participation in numerous political conferences, seminars and meetings.

In concluding, I would like to reiterate that I generally consider myself a manager or an administrator, rather than a professional, since I do not have any academic or 'formal' credentials to be proud of. On the other hand, however, I have gradually come to believe that academic or formal qualifications are not sufficient for developing tangible competences. In my opinion, real or concrete competences are those capabilities that empower people to accomplish various tasks efficiently and effectively and these take form in the intricate interplay between education/training, practice/experience and critical thinking or reflection. Incidentally, in this era of globalization and ICT, which have entailed fundamental changes in the nature and modalities of education itself, I think it is high time that institutions of higher education devised appropriate mechanisms for dealing with the recognition of prior and experiential learning, so as to establish up–to–date, rational and fair criteria and standards for concrete competences.

III. Teachers in Exile

Hungry for Education - Dreams from my Mother

By Girmai Gebrehiwet Azbeha

I was born in the early '50s in a town called Nefasit in Northern Red Sea Zone. I started my elementary level education in 1959. Since Eritrea at that time was under federal rule with Ethiopia I started my elementary education in Tigrigna (my mother tongue), but later on it was changed to Amharic which is alien language for Eritrean citizens. The education system for elementary level was 1-4 and for junior 5-8, but after Ethiopia annexed Eritrea it was changed to 1-6 for elementary and 7-8 Junior. I sat for General Examination in 6th and 8th and I passed in both examinations and proceeded to secondary level.

I was forced to transfer to Asmara, capital city of Eritrea to continue my education from junior level onwards, because at that time Nefasit School was only up to elementary level. I used to stay alone in Asmara by renting a single room. Nefasit is 25 kilometres away from Asmara that lies on the route to Massawa. My mother used to send me food daily by bus. It was a hard time for me and my mother, because it was not easy to send daily a bag of food and it was also not satisfactory enough for me, because it was not enough and tasty. However, what made me continue my study was by my mother's determination and encouragement. She was illiterate, but a very dedicated and visionary mother who always checked my exercise books and tried to fulfil what I needed as much as she could.

Eritrean politics at that time was very popular. As a youngster I used to hear about the army struggle and observed how the Eritrean people suffered from the Ethiopian army. Villages were burned, people in rural and urban areas were massacred and their belongings like cattle, sheep, and camels etc. were brutally killed. Night curfew and other controlling mechanisms were implemented everyday and everywhere. This situation has influenced the youngsters to develop more hatred and sentiment of opposition to the ruling regime.

The education system of Ethiopia was not in favour of Eritreans. Amharic as a language of the coloniser became the medium of instruction in elementary level and as a language compulsory in all other proceeding levels. To continue higher education everyone had to pass in Amharic. These preconditions became hindrance for Eritreans to participate in higher education, because Amharic is a foreign and unpopular language for Eritreans. In contrary, books that were written in Eritrean languages were burned and banned for print. As part of the society it was a challenge for my continuation in academic education. The situation was a dilemma for me whether to join the army struggle as a means of opposition to the oppression of Ethiopia or to continue my academic education. Finally, I managed to complete my secondary education tolerating all sorts of problems that encountered me.

After completing my secondary level academic education in Asmara in 1970 I joined Haile Selassie Teacher Training Institute in Kotebe/Addis Ababa in 1972.

I worked as elementary level teacher in southern part of Ethiopia in a region named Elubabour in a village called Masha. After serving as a teacher for two years, I joined the Eritrean army struggle in 1975. After taking military training I was assigned in Social Affairs Department especially in Education Division. I worked as a member of a mobile unit as a coordinator and supervisor in different parts of Eritrea until 1978. Our main task was to move around villages and study conditions that allowed us to open education centres that could be run by the community. To participate militarily whenever and where ever necessary was part of our obligation. I participated in a battle that was planned to liberate a city in southern part of Eritrea called Adi

Keyh and my leg was injured there. After taking treatment I was assigned in base area as a teacher in boarding school located in a place called Sahel that caters children of nomadic families, kids of the fighters and children who were displaced because of the war. In 1979 I was assigned as an elementary school director in a liberated city called Keren until the front retreated strategically to the base area, because of Soviet military intervention as a backer for the Ethiopian regime. Meanwhile, I was assigned to the Sudan, Kessala as an elementary school director and gradually as coordinator of the four schools that were gradually opened in that area which were meant to serve Eritrean refugees residing there. I served in Kessala, Sudan for eight years until 1988.

Kessala is a big boarder city in which a huge number of Eritrean refugees settled and it was the centre of different Eritrean army struggle organisation's head offices. As a reflection of the internal conflict of the liberation organisations there was serious tension and division among Eritrean refugees there. The different groups were using the schools as means of influencing the people and attracting followers and sympathisers. In such situation the effort of our school was to admit any Eritrean citizens regardless of their families' political background and to create a condition of confidence for the parents by producing best performing students and drawing them to participate in their children's educational affairs. Thanks to the team of teachers who put their utmost effort to capture the hearts and needs of the parents in which finally we were able to grow our influence that enabled us to open up to four schools. In addition to the influence we gained by the school activities we introduced extra curricular activities that attracted almost the majority of the youngsters residing in the city. It was a great achievement to see most Eritrean youth in refugee situation to gather in activities that participated peacefully regardless their political sentiment. Since I was leading the activity I consider it one of the best achievements I recorded.

As a product of our schools' exertion our students competed in various activities against other Eritrean refugees living in other parts of Sudan. Our schools in Kessala not only benefited in producing a situation of harmony and coherence among Eritreans residing there, but also created a favourable condition to live in peace and pleasant relationship with the host country's people and government of the Sudan.

Series of assessment meetings and seminars that focused on parents, students and school relationships were conducted. The relationship between parents, students and teachers was very tight. Students organised various club activities like arts, drama, literature, music, dance, sports etc. and showed their products to the parents. Parents were actively participating in solving problems that the schools faced. They contributed financially and participated physically in building extra classrooms and maintenance works. Teachers were visiting student's homes in occasions when there happened to be any discipline problems or academic weaknesses and on occasions of religious or family importance. The relationship developed between students, parents and teachers on that instances remained warm and lives until these days. At this moment I feel proud and content when I see my previous refugee students are among the graduates from higher education; skilful experts in different sectors of the independent nation Eritrea.

Different short courses and workshops were conducted at central and school level. There were occasions where Eritrean scholars and experts came from different parts of Diasporas to the liberated base area to conduct seminars. I participated in seminars that were conducted by Dr. Teame who was professor of education in the University of Bristol, UK and another. At different occasions seminars were conducted by Dr. Bereket who was professor of education in the University of Lund, Sweden. The seminar was mainly about curriculum designing and assessment, pedagogy, education philosophy, supervision, administration and planning of education etc.

In 1989 I served as a school director in Sahel Zero boarding school. Then after the liberation of the Southern Region of Eritrea, I served as school director and coordinator of school found in Adi Keyh. The schools that I was administering then in Keren and Adi Keyh were operating during night because they were under enemy military planes threat. However, Eritrea liberated in May 1991 in which the situation of terror and oppression was changed into a new era of prosperity and hope.

After the independence of Eritrea I was assigned in Denkalia Region as a Regional Education Office Head in September 1991 and served there up to 1996. Denkalia is a vast region whose education provision was very scarce and limited to the port city Assab and its surroundings. The inhabitants of Denkalia are from Afar ethnic group in which most of them depend on nomadic life and very few on fishery and merchandising. The challenges which we had were: firstly, to open schools in the central area of the dispersed nomadic people houses, secondly, to introduce education in mother tongue in order to accommodate most of the people and third, to sensitize the people to allow girls to participate in education. During my stay in Denkalia I was really satisfied with the fact that I observed better access and more male students' participants and better acceptance of Afar language as mother tongue medium of instruction in elementary level. Meanwhile, girls' participation is still a serious setback in Denkalia Region especially in rural areas.

In the beginning of 1993, a workshop was organised by the MoE in Asmara. That training was the fist of its kind after liberation of Eritrea. The content of the training was almost the same as what I have learned from Dr. Teame's and Dr. Bereket's seminars during the struggle era. However, with the new situation of liberation the later workshop content and presentation was much more relevant because it was presented in association with the new development of the nation.

During my stay in Denkalia in 1993, I got a short scholarship in the University of Birmingham UK to attend for post graduate certificate in education. As part of the study I visited a number of schools that teach students of different social and economic status. It was my first time to visit schools that are stratified and organised according to social backgrounds. I visited schools which accommodate refugees who came from Afghanistan and Iraq etc. who were not able to adjust to the new cultural and economical situation. I also visited schools in which most of the students' parents were either workers or unemployed. I visited a school in which students' parents are owners of big farmland, industry and some higher officials of the government including one African youngster's parent who is the president of one African state. The school fee which one student pays was estimated by one Kenyan colleague as the yearly budget of one of the boarding schools in his country. The notion that says "value added" was very striking to my thinking and believe. The idea that relates students from poor economic and social background to less intelligence I heard there conflicted with the purpose of education which is development and change of the practical situation so that students from poor families and disadvantaged social backgrounds can achieve a higher education and sometimes excel all others. Since it was my first time to visit Europe I really admired the development and wished Eritrea, my country, to reach that stage. I used that opportunity to visit my relatives who were in Germany and Holland and returned back home.

Government of Eritrea reorganised the Eritrean administrative regions from eight to six zobas. After the reorganisation I was assigned as Northern Red Sea Zoba Education Office Head in 1996. I stayed in Northern Red Sea Zoba until August 1998. Northern Red Sea is a zoba that has five ethnic groups who organise the education provision in mother tongue very complicated. In Northern Red Sea Zone I got the chance of scholarship training from the MoE, to participate in Paris, France in the International Institute for Educational Planning (IIEP) from September 1998 up to May 1999. My training was mainly on educational planning and administration. In addition, study visits were organised and conducted in regions of France and in Japan for ten days. In addition to the tour we conducted in various levels of education and big machine factories and made discussion meetings with leaders and managers of education institutes and industries. We managed to meet the Minister of Education of Japan and get briefings about the education system of Japan.

After I returned home, I was assigned as Zoba Maekel Education Office Head from 1999 for four years. Zoba Maekel is a zoba in which the capital city Asmara is located. There are seven administrative sub zobas. Four of them are inside Asmara and the remaining three are in suburbs of Asmara. Schools of all levels are very concentrated in Asmara that the rural area. There is great pressure to administer the schools inside Asmara, because of the assembly in a very small area. However, there is an advantage of availability of many demands. In 2000 the government of Eritrea has initiated in collaboration donors a project that focuses on Early Childhood Development (ECD). The project was designed and implemented by sectors like health, or social welfare that have interest in different aspects of a child and mother. As part of the project I got the chance of a study visit to Kenya and South Africa in December 2001. The lesson I learned from this tour was very fruitful. The multi-sectoral integrated approach project has developed the zoba in increasing access and finding different approaches to train and accommodate teachers and kids respectively.

In late 2003 I was assigned to Warsay Ykealo School, Sawa. It was a great challenge to establish such a complex school, because the administration structure was not comprehensively formed and there was not enough administration manpower to run the school. Warsay Ykealo School is a special school that caters 12th grade students gathered from all Secondary School in the nation. Students from all ethnic groups who have a variety of cultural and academic backgrounds are expected to share their experience and come up with similar value and national harmony. Every year at an average of 12,000 to 19,000 students attend in Warsay Ykealo boarding School. Students sit for Eritrean Secondary School Leaving Certificate Examination (ESSLC). Those who pass the examination join higher education and the others join skill developing trainings. The focus of administration in such school is different from other schools. The main target is to prepare the students for the final national examination. One of the advantage the youngsters benefit from is experience in self-help practices and exchange of culture and life experience among each other since it is their first incident to be away from their family.

After four scholastic years I was transferred to Zoba Maekel as Education Office Head in 2007. Relatively Zoba Maekel is one of the best advantaged zobas which have good access in all levels of education. Currently it focuses on developing the quality of education. In order to guarantee better academic achievement and highly disciplined citizens, schools are working hard to encourage parents to pay attention and intent to their children's education and teachers are given intensive professional training, school based supervision is intensified etc. Health education is part of building the holistic personality of a citizen. The MoE focuses on school health issues by giving training and providing health facilities.

I tried to discuss my social, political and professional background so that the reader is able to comprehend and justify the real situation I have come up from. As I have mentioned earlier I have attended various training programmes that helped me in my job. I have worked in education at different levels of administration. Generally I can say that I am confident and satisfied with the effort I put in and the outcome obtained. There is no situation of regret that I feel concerning my career. However, I recognise the fact that the opportunity to continue studying and get a certification is something that I miss. In the army struggle anyone who fits for the obligation is engaged; there is no need to forward a certificate. But in the world system that we are now in certification is very vital. The experience I collected in this long journey needs to be systematically organised and related to the world's education system; to be refined and strengthened by learning from it. Though I had chances of trainings it was not standardised and accredited as per time spent and learned content.

The opportunity I got to attend in distance learning seems to me as the chance I got to fill the gap I have missed due to the situation I have already disclosed. So far I found the programme very interesting and I hope to succeed. I really thank the University of Kaiserslautern for the effort they put to offer mechanism that accommodates for individuals like me to move forward together.

As I have already mentioned earlier I joined the liberation struggle in 1975. Being a member of armed struggle all directions and guidelines were passed on as military orders. All the duties and tasks one accomplishes during the army struggle did not require bureaucratic procedure, it was order that passed from leadership and everyone had to implement it in any kind of job. Since I was part of that system, I participated as a soldier, served as a teacher, director, coordinator and regional education head in different parts of Eritrea. In all jobs and obligations I participated in different positions; I did not write certificates or letters. However, as a record of participation every member of the Liberation Front keeps it in the form of table report.

Teaching during the Armed Struggle

By Hailu Asfaha Foto

This document reflects the development of my entire competence. It provides my detailed background since my childhood. It elaborates my educational background as well as my work experiences in various areas of responsibility I have pursued. In addition, I have tried to include my reflections with regard to the studies I have pursued in various higher educational institutions in Eritrea as well as in other countries.

I was born in December 27, 1956 in a small town called Maihabar, Eritrea. As I reached the age of schooling I started 1st grade education in Asmara, the capital city of Eritrea. Then together with my family moved to Ethiopia and continued my education grades 2-4 in a town called Gonder. After I completed grade four we returned to Eritrea and continued my elementary, middle and secondary levels of education that is grades 5-12 in a town called Dekemhare. In 1974, I took the then National Secondary School Leaving Examination.

After I passed the Ethiopian Secondary School Leaving Examination (ESLE) I was prepared to go to Ethiopia to pursue my higher education in the University of Addis Ababa. However, in 1974 there was a regime change in Ethiopia. A military junta came to power overthrowing Emperor Haile Selassie who ruled Ethiopia for about 40 years. At that time the new regime continued and intensified the atrocities against the Eritrean people, especially targeting at the youth. This situation enhanced nationalism and compelled the youth to join the armed struggle to fight against the colonial regime for independence. I, together with my friends and classmates were influenced by the situation and decided to join the struggle for independence. As a result I abandoned the ambition I had to continue my education at higher education and joined the armed struggle in 1975.

Experience In the Struggle for Liberation From 1975-1991

It is to be recalled that Eritrea was annexed with Ethiopia in 1962. One year prior to the annexation, due to the oppression carried out by the Ethiopian regime, the Eritrean people have started armed struggle for the liberation of independent Eritrea in September 1961. The armed struggle gained huge support from the Eritrean people and many Eritreans from various walks of life joined the struggle for liberation to fight against the Ethiopian colonization. I as an Eritrean together with my friends as well as classmates was also influenced by the struggle for independence and joined the armed struggle in 1975.

After having military and political training, I was assigned to the front line as a fighter. During 1975 up to mid 1978 I was fighting in the front line against the Ethiopian army. I was wounded at my leg in mid 1978. Following my treatment in the fronts' hospital I was assigned to be a teacher in the Eritrean Peoples Liberation Front (EPLF) Department of Education which was in charge of education during the period of the armed struggle.

Experience as a Teacher in the Liberated Area

In 1976, the EPLF has established a Department of Education in the liberated areas. The major idea was to lead and coordinate all educational activities all over the front line for the fighters as well as for the civilian population in the liberated areas. Fighters from all over the front who had been teachers before they joined the armed struggle and those who had higher educational qualification were summoned to establish the Department of Education. A structure was drawn and relevant branches such as curriculum, research, teacher training etc. were established to commence the various educational activities. Then after, curriculum and teacher training manuals were developed. Those fighters who were deployed to be teachers received their initial teacher training programme in pedagogy and upbringing and assigned as teachers to commence teaching children. A centre was established which was called the Revolution School (Zero School).

After I joined the Revolution School I was also trained together with my colleagues for two months on pedagogy and upbringing. Having teaching practice for a week I was assigned to teach at elementary level. That was my first experience as a teacher in teaching at elementary level in the Revolution School for two months.

Experience In the Sudan As a Teacher and School Director

The 1960s and 70s were remembered as the worst time in the history of Eritrea. Sever atrocities were committed by the Ethiopian army against the people of Eritrea. Many Eritrean villages were burned into ashes and thousands of people were massacred indiscriminately. During those times there was a slogan used by the Ethiopian regime which said "to annihilate the fish drain the water", meaning you had to annihilate the source, which is the Eritrean people, to destroy the liberation struggle. To implement this slogan the Ethiopian army has committed many atrocities against the people of Eritrea. They killed thousands of Eritrean people including children and women. As a result, the Eritrean people were forced to flee in tens of thousands to the Sudan to save their lives.

As part of its political activity, EPLF took a measure to provide social service, mainly education for the Eritrean refugees in the Sudan. Eritreans who migrated in tens of thousands, lived in various refugee camps as well as in towns in Sudan.

In 1980, me and some colleagues were assigned in the Sudan to open schools for the Eritrean refugees. My first placement was in Gedarif, a town which is found in the eastern part of the Sudan, to serve as a teacher. It was my first experience to teach in a formally established elementary school which eventually created me an opportunity to develop and acquire more knowledge and skills in the teaching learning process. After having fulfilled my duty and responsibility as a teacher for one academic year in 1980, I was promoted to be a school director in the same school.

Eritreans who were in Gedarif came in large number to register their children, after the opening of the school was announced. This was a good opportunity for me to teach Eritrean children outside my country. During my stay in Gedarif until 1985, I have been diligently working in organizing and managing various educational activities. Besides, I have prepared and lead numerous cultural activities for the children as well as for the communities in order to create awareness in educational, social and cultural affairs.

In addition, I organized a meeting for parents and other members of the Eritrean community to discuss various educational issues and to elect a Parent Teacher Association (PTA). This association was democratically elected by the people. I organised and conducted regular meetings with members of PTA to discuss on various school management and educational issues. The PTA was highly committed and worked to mobilise the parents and other community members to send their children to the school. Moreover, they have mobilised the people to contribute to the development of the school in the form of financial, labour and material support. As a result, the community has consistently contributed the support required to alleviate the challenges of the school.

After successfully finishing my duties and responsibilities as a director for four years, I was transferred to a refugee camp called Sebea which is located in the central part of the Sudan. It was my first experience to work in a refugee camp and this really became a great opportunity for me to understand and learn from the social, cultural and economic situation of the refugee community. Nevertheless, regardless of their alienation from their country and the severe economic problems they were facing, they were determined to send their children to school. Me as a school director, on top of my responsibility to lead the educational activity, I have also organised teachers and students to collaborate with the refugees and assist them in their agricultural fields during ploughing and harvesting period. This activity has been done continuously including other various aspects of their social and cultural life. It has an effect to attract the hearts and minds of the people and influence them in return to actively collaborate with the school.

My final experience in the Sudan was in Khartoum the capital city of Sudan. In 1986, I was assigned to Khartoum to open a new school for the Eritrean refugees. Prior to the opening of the school, I organised and conducted intensive consultation meetings with the Eritrean community to clarify and make them understand the objectives in opening a school in Khartoum and the roles expected from them to play in the establishment of the school. Firstly, the community was delighted that their children had the opportunity to get education. Secondly, they showed their dedication and commitment to actively participate in the establishment of the school. Then the community was organised in various committees according to their profession, such as construction workers, carpenters, plumbers, traders etc. This was deliberately made with the consent of the people in order to involve them in the establishment of the school based on their profession. A campaign was launched through these committees to create awareness on the communities and involve them in the construction of various school facilities. After finalising the preparation, people participated in the construction of classrooms, in the making of students' tables, blackboards, and in collecting financial contribution. After one year of intensive preparation the school was opened in 1987. We initially started to teach elementary level students. However, the demand for middle level education was enormous. Taking the necessity of the demand into consideration the school was upgraded to middle level in 1989.

Moreover, the community has also demanded to start an education programme for adults during evening hours. In Khartoum there were thousands of young people and adults who have not got the opportunity to go to school. Hence, it was envisaged the importance of adult education programme and a study was carried out. Finally, I opened the adult education programme which offered from grade one to grade three.

I worked in Khartoum until the academic year 1991/92 that has contributed a lot to develop my experience in teaching, managing schools as well as working with the community.

Experience Post Eritrea's Independence

Following the independence of Eritrea in 1991, I had the opportunity to sit the National examination for the Eritrean Secondary Education Certificate Examination (ESECE). I passed the exam and joined the University of Asmara after 17 years of absence from education and successfully completed my second year education at the University. However, I was assigned in the Department of Planning in the Ministry of Education in 1993. Due to this I was compelled to interrupt my study at university and was engaged only in my new post.

After working for one year as a planner I was again promoted to be the head of the Southern Region Education Office, (1994-2000). Southern Region is one of the most populated regions in Eritrea. It was a challenging task for me to be the head of the regional education office. The region is very wide and densely populated; it had more than 200 educational institutions with more than 2000 teachers. However, the experience I had acquired during the liberation struggle as a teacher and school director in the Sudan, a planner in the Ministry of Education and the two years education I attended the University of Asmara has provided me the necessary knowledge and skill in managing of educational services effectively and efficiently.

My main responsibility as regional education officer was to lead the overall educational services in the Southern Region. During my stay in that region from 1994 to 2000 I have diligently worked to expand access to education and enhance quality of education. Targeting remote areas and disadvantaged communi-

88

ties I opened many schools. I have also developed and implemented a plan that will guide to a gradual achievement of universal primary education and the expansion of secondary education. As a result access to and quality of education have considerably improved.

Besides, I have designed and established a cluster management system whereby teachers and school directors regularly meet and discuss on various educational affairs. Training programmes were also organised and conducted for teachers to raise their competence in teaching. School directors have also provided training on various educational management issues. Besides, teachers and directors of the same cluster conduct regular meetings to share best practices among themselves. Eventually, this clusters changed into Pedagogic Resource Centres (PRCs) to serve as resource centres for both teachers and school directors of the cluster schools.

Since 1979, I have been working in different areas of responsibility in the education sector. From 1979 up to 1981 I have worked as a teacher and from 1992 up to1992 as a school director. The detailed experience I had during my career as a teacher and school director is mentioned above.

Following the independence of Eritrea in 1991, I was assigned in 1993 in the Department of Planning in the Ministry of Education as a planner. In 1994, I was promoted to be a regional education head in Southern Region and worked up to 2000.

While fulfilling my duties and responsibilities as regional education officer I got the opportunity of further education for one year on advanced educational planning and management training at the International Institute for Educational Planning (IIEP), Paris, France. After successfully finishing my training and awarding international diploma in 2001, I was promoted to be the Director of Research and Statistics Division in the Ministry of Education and I am currently holding that post.

Since 2001 as a director I have been actively engaged in designing, implementing and monitoring of various projects supported by World Band (WB), African Development Bank (ADB), the European Commission (EC) and the United Nations Children's Fund (UNICEF). As part of the project I have also worked as a counter part with various national and international consultants.

Furthermore, since 2001 till now, I have been working till now as a chair person of the Technical Committee for "Education For All" (EFA). During the past 10 years I have developed together with my colleagues the National Education for All Framework for Action and organised regional and national consultation workshops. I have also assisted regional education offices in the assessment of Education for All as well as in developing the regional EFA Framework for Action of their respective regions. Currently, I am working to carry out an end-decade assessment of EFA.

Participation in Continuing Training

In 1997 I got an opportunity to further continue my higher education in India. I joined the National Institute of Educational Planning and Administration (NIEPA), New Delhi, India. After attending a three month intensive training in the institute I carried out a three month intensive research work and prepared a research paper titled "A study of quality secondary schooling in Southern Region in Eritrea" and submitted it to the institute to fulfil the requirement. Finally, I was awarded an International Diploma on Educational Planning and Administration from NIEPA.

Following my completion of the diploma programme I went back to my previous post head of the Southern Region Education Office. The scientific knowledge and skill I acquired from the training in educational planning and administration, in India has significantly contributed to further develop my personal practical knowledge. It has also an impact on improving my leadership capacity to manage the educational activities in the region more systematically and competently. I have also shared the knowledge and skill I acquired from the training with my colleagues and significantly contributed to improve their work performance.

In 2000, I have also got another opportunity to pursue my higher education in Paris, France. I joined the International Institute for Educational Planning (IIEP) for advanced training on educational planning and management from September 2000-2001. The main training programme components were common core subjects such as policy formulation and strategic planning in education, education sector diagnosis, the use of simulation model in planning educational provision, from policy to action: feasibility testing, financing and information systems (EMIS).

The second component was on specialised modules such as Compulsory Course on Strategic Issues in Educational Development, Designing Educational Development Projects and Monitoring and Evaluating the Quality of Education. After successfully completing the intensive training programme I did my research thesis on a title "The retention and quality of secondary school students in Southern Region" and finally awarded an international diploma.

Following my completion of the IIEP advanced training programme in 2001, I was promoted to a new job as the Director of Research and Statistics Division in the central Ministry of Education. Since then I have been actively working in leading the division and coordinating various projects and research activities.

It is worth noting that the higher education I have perused in NIEPA, India and IIEP, France in advanced educational planning and administration have significantly contributed to gain scientific knowledge and be able to translate it into practical knowledge for practice through education officers, school directors and teachers. Moreover, it had an impact for my current job to competently manage the responsibilities I have and lead effectively various projects and programmes as a coordinator, programmer and researcher.

Finally, I would like to reflect on the current further higher education I am pursuing through distance learning in the University of Kaiserslautern. I am one of the members of the Ministry of Education currently attending the master studies programme "School Management".

Although I had the chance to continue my higher education in NIEPA and IIEP on Educational Planning and Administration that has contributed a lot to my knowledge and skill, I considered the current programme on school management more inspiring and practical to adapt to the situation in Eritrea. After following the programme for almost two years I feel comfortable that I could be able to understand the various terms and concepts related to school development.

More specifically, now I will confidently say that I acquired in depth the scientific knowledge on pedagogy and school development, learning culture and project management, leadership styles and their contribution to the development of organisation and society, concepts and methods of organisational development, teaching quality and assessment of quality learning, team building and communication, human resource and school development, quality management and educational research. This programme has significantly contributed to develop my competence on the above mentioned fields of knowledge and subsequently enhanced my capacity to translate it into practical knowledge in my future career.

Education During War: The EPLF as a Learning Organisation

By Tquabo Aimut Gebreselassie

In the village where I was brought up, it was not possible to find any evidence or role model as an outcome of modern education and training as a reference almost 45 years ago. It was completely an illiterate environment far from any sign of modern or urban products. It may be surprising to say that I had not even seen any type of locomotive until I completed grade four and moved to a town very far from where my parents lived to continue my education.

A school with two rooms and two teachers were the only signs of my future hope in that particular village called Sarda. The wish and action of my parents to send me to this historical school so as to be a good kid grown as an 'educated person' was a great opportunity where only very few children were privileged to partake of in that particular area. My parent's decision to have them a better educated son, of high expectation and value, leading a different life from theirs, serves as a potential driving force to pursue my academic education in a manner of accepted behaviour and good performance. It is to say that my parent's grand expectation and the way I was brought up had great influence on my overall behaviour and personal characteristics during my students life.

I did my junior and secondary school studies in two different towns very far from my own village in a different environment characterized by fear, discrimination and uncertainty for the reason that Eritrea was then colonised by Ethiopia. At about the age of 12 years old child, it was not easy for me to manag life as a pupil in such an unfriendly environment with no close relative to rely on.

Once I completed my secondary school and almost with no or very little work experience I decided to join the armed struggle for independence in the Eritrean People's Liberation Front (EPLF) in 1975 rather than to go to Addis Ababa- Ethiopia to continue my tertiary education. The Eritrean Peoples Liberation Front is an Eritrean organisation that lead the Eritrean people in the achievement of its hard won independence in 1991.

Along the mandate of fighting the enemy as a soldier carrying a gun, assisting non-literate fighters to be able to read and write was one of the common activities among the fighters guided by the general orientation 'The literate must teach and the non- literate must learn'. This was my initial experience of teaching the literacy in mother tongue for the first time in the field for individual learners. Intensive informal education through different media was highly practiced and was instrumental in raising the consciousness and critical thinking of the target audiences including the freedom fighters.

Except the initial two years serving as a soldier carrying a gun at the front line, my whole experience in the armed struggle as member of the EPLF had been of civil service and particularly as a teacher and elementary school director in the education section. The competencies developed afterwards were deeply founded in my experience and attitude that I developed during 16 years as a freedom fighter. Despite the paramount hardships and miserable circumstances, the EPLF was really like a well established and effective learning organisation in terms of social, cultural and political orientations for the fighters who wholeheartedly accepted its goal: the total independence of Eritrea. I joined at the early period of my adolescent age for which I was highly influenced by the thoughts and principles of my organisation mostly self–reliance and social justice among others.

Competencies developed during the armed struggle were something that can be defined or explained as comprehensive and all rounded which included: emotional competencies with good skills of common sense, conflict management, collaborative work and eagerness to learn from the experience of others. Moreover, core values as tolerance, mutual respect and trust as well as practical social skills including creativity and innovation were the results learned and acquired on the basis of the principles of social justice and self-reliance.

Apart from the short time working as a soldier my first civil work was "teaching" with no sound training in pedagogy and related concepts. As a freedom fighter the only option I had, was to accept this and work hard to meet the requirements. The sentiment or attitude expressed as "since I'm entrusted to do this job, I will not quit, I will do it" was the mental determination, all members of the community of freedom fighters expected to inherit and develop.

The main competencies I developed during the armed struggle (apart from limited military knowledge and skills) were teaching small kids and managing an elementary school as a school director. As I have already indicated, I had not a pinch of idea how to teach kids or manage a school except the experience which I noted of what good teachers do and how a director administered a school in my past years as a student. However, the important factor I dedicated myself to, was to be a faithful and responsible person, as my parents as well as my organisation taught me, and implement whatever was expected and bestowed upon me.

All these positive expectations and constructive environments of my experience in the armed struggle for independence laid solid foundations for my career development as a civil servant. They also helped me to develop competencies related to teaching and school management as well as socio-cultural and political orientations towards a culture of unity in diversity, tolerance and of living and working in harmony.

In 1991 Eritrea was liberated and officially became independent in 1993. Although there was no real difference in-terms of ideology and developmental principles, the main goal once Eritrea got its independence was totally different and demanded a nation building that required different institutional working conditions and competencies to provide efficient and effective services in all sectors. One of the critical challenges was therefore, to assess already acquired and developed competencies as an armed struggle fighter with the given institutional and civil life working culture. Immediately after independence I started thinking which profession to develop. This was a challenge and very difficult to decide at that time. First I was interested to devote myself to the field of "counselling and guidance" to give career developments professional support and advice to secondary school students. I had more than 13 years experience of teaching with a good knowledge of teaching, performance evaluation, school management, working relation with parents and community as well programme planning and evaluation.

At this juncture I opted to pursue my higher education and joined Asmara University in 1993 to upgrade and enhance my educational level in line to my long working experiences. Due to health problem, however, I withdrew from my study. Anyway I was left with the impression and awareness of the need to improve my professional capacity in order to work competently in the new environment of nation building

Despite the unfavourable conditions of life and work during the armed struggle, a healthy spirit of 'I can do it' mentality helped me to go on. Although my dream was to study about counselling and guidance, I joined Adult Education Section in 1994, a new area that I had very little experience. One year later I got chance to attend a three month course of the International Adult Education Institute in 1994 in India. This was really an encouraging and promising occasion and a turning point for me to be interested in the field of adult education as a profession. This was followed by a two year course of Diploma on Adult Education

(1995-1997) with detailed and comprehensive adult education courses in Tanzania. This course was useful to me for the fact that I had about two year experience as an adult education staff and I was able to identify my learning needs in line to the mandate I was expected to perform competently and professionally. As the result of the opportunity to attend the above mentioned short and long training courses on adult education, I was able to identify and address important strategic areas such as: how to introduce adult education projects or programmes and how to manage it; how to support adult education staff to be efficient and effective in their work; how to develop curriculum and instructional materials as well as how to get and manage appropriate data etc.

Adult education was provided during the armed struggle by EPLF. After independence, it was since 2000 that adult and non-formal education started to be expanded as a programme. This demanded planning and management skills and in line to this I got chance to participate in a one year "Educational Planning and Management Programme" of IIEP in Paris in 2000. This helped me to reflect on my experience, enhance my understanding of educational planning and management and get a broad understanding of the course. It helped me to act professionally in specific areas.

Since 2003 I have been assigned as the Division Head of Curriculum Planning and Development for adult and non-formal education in Eritrea. The skills and competencies I developed then are more related with curriculum development and preparation of instructional materials, conducting learning needs assessment and research as well as development of policy and strategic documents in collaboration with local as well as international consultants.

New Eritrea is the product of a protracted and demanding long armed struggle for independence costing invaluable human and material resources. Despite the huge challenges and destructive war thanks to EPLF that important lessons had been learned and useful competences developed by the Eritrean citizens that can be applied in nation building and self –development. As Peter Senge indicated in his concept of "learning organisation", I found EPLF meets all the criteria of his definition for which all the fighters and those civilians working undercover, were able to smartly face whatever challenge and come up successfully. Developing emotional, social and political competencies were among the requirements developed in order to be able to survive in such unfavourable and challenging situations. As a member of the organisation, I was able to develop such important competencies as to act efficiently and competently and I can also say this serves me as a foundation to my current working condition as an adult educator.

EPLF was a unique freedom fighting organisation, not only because of its military and leadership capacity but also as a learning organisation that tried to apply the three fields of education: formal, non-formal and informal domains as far as possible in the difficult situations that mostly defined as 'Fighting against all odds' natural as well as manmade. Important lessons can be explored out of the rich experience under the given title 'Education and war': EPLF's experience for education system in general and how to maximize the application of informal and non-formal education in particular for equitable and sustainable development.

As a way forward, I would like to emphasis on the need to sustain, enhance and update my current competencies along the lines of my expected roles and responsibilities: as a married man and father of three kids to continue a happy and coherent family life; as a citizen to continue serving my country faithfully; as a worker to act responsibly and professionally; and as a lifelong learner, to revise and improve my competencies and learning style continuously based on the principles of adult education: self-directing and purposeful self-study in order to remain updated and informed.

Struggle for Education and Independence

By Yossif Tewelde Negusse

It is understood that every person has his/her own pedagogic experience. If I am to describe my experience since my childhood education, I started at a church school reciting religious texts since there were no kindergarten schools at that time. There I was able to read and write Tigrigna alphabets and started directly second grade when I got a chance to enter into a nearby government school at elementary level. At that time it was very difficult to enter government schools, because there were very few schools and too many school age children to be enrolled. Thus, children were made to draw lotteries in order to get a chance to start schooling. If one is unfortunate he or she needs to wait for the next year. I myself had missed one year, but the next year, fortunately my younger brother got the chance and my father agreed with the director of the school to substitute me instead of my brother.

Education was being offered for free. Once you got the chance to enter a government school, there was no problem to continue even if you were from a poor family. Everything, such as stationery, books and even breakfast were being offered by the government. Since I started schooling until grade ten, I was a prize winner.

In my study skills, I didn't like subjects which insisted memorization, such as history and geography. In general, I liked science subjects and in particular physical sciences. However, I was a voracious reader. I liked reading reference books other than the student textbooks given for the grade thereby getting a co hensive understanding of the subjects we were learning. In tion, I read newspapers and magazines daily. My father was an addicted person of newspapers. He brought home a newspaper daily. Thus, I became addicted too. As for the other reading materials, I went to the library. At that time, there were three public libraries in Asmara other than the school libraries. There was this American Library, which was then called USIS (United States Information Service) and now is called Asmara Public Library, the British Council Library which still is serving as it is and a public library owned by the government, posted in the building of the Ministry of Education (MoE). All these libraries were open from 8:00 a.m. to 8:00 p.m. to everybody who wanted to read and use them. Anybody could also borrow books if he issued a borrowing card. Since we were going to school in both the morning and afternoon shifts I was using the library after school from 5:00 to 8:00 pm. and on Saturdays. I was also borrowing books to read at home.

At the end of 8th Grade I sat for the General National Examination and passed with a very high mark and joined the then called Prince Makonnen Secondary School, now Asmara Comprehensive Secondary School. Most of the high mark scorer students were being sent to this school at that time. At my high school years, since there were many competitors, I couldn't manage to stand first prize and in both grades nine and ten I stood third. In grade 11 and 12 still lagged behind. At that time, my father was insisting either to join Teacher Training Institute or Nursing School so that I could help him by getting a job early and earn a salary. But my goal was to finish my college education. So, although many courses were being offered for a quick-fix, I insisted to continue my high school education. My younger brother couldn't resist it and so from grade 10 on he joined the Ethiopian Air Force to become a pilot. I myself after sitting for the examination at the end of grade 12, although I was dead sure to pass the examination and join the Haile Selassie University in Addis Ababa, which was the only university at that time, decided to join the Ethiopian Navy. I had two reasons to take this decision. First, I knew that my father would not allow me to continue my education by any means. I had to get a job and help him. Second, I thought that if I joined the navy, it would be easy to get a scholarship to a foreign country. Unfortunately, as soon as I joined the navy, I realised that those who should go for a scholarship were already selected in Addis Ababa. Thus, my dream of getting a scholarship failed. On the other hand, I was informed that I successfully passed the matriculation to join the university.

To tell about my results of the examination, there were subjects which do not need much effort to memorize: To all-sided surprise, I was the only one who did not choose biology for the examination out of 80 grade twelve students in the school. The biology teacher was always asking my classmates when I left class during the biology period by saying "What happened to the boy? Is he sick?" because at that time, biology was the easiest subject to score, if you had the capacity to memorise all the jargon terms and every student was taking it as if it was a compulsory subject.

Anyhow, after I understood that I won't have the chance of scholarship to a foreign country and heard that I scored well in this examination, I and my friend who had the same idea decided to leave the military camp secretly. At that time once you were recruited to the military, there was no way to get out of it. I and my friend had already two months of military training. If we asked for withdrawal officially, they would not have allowed us. Instead, they would have taken us to prison considering that we came for espionage for the ELF. Fortunately, we managed to get out of it and came back home. When we came out the deadline for registration time to join the university had already passed. The only chance we had was to pay 30 Ethiopian Dollars for late registration. My friend was able to pay and join the university but my father was not willing to pay for me and so I missed that year.

Nevertheless, I never stopped dreaming of joining the university and get at least my bachelor degree. In order to fulfil this I had to find a job and save money. In the first three months of that year, I worked as a team leader of nine members for a population census conducted in Massawa and Assab towns sponsored by the Eritrean administration. A similar two teams were also sent to the other Eritrean towns. After finishing this task, I was employed by the Department of Education on a status of direct teaching with a salary of 120 Eth. Dollars a month. When schools were closed for the summer vacation, I was selected to take the First Summer Course of Teacher Education at Debreberhan Teacher Training Institute which is about 80 km. from Addis Ababa.

After taking this course, I applied to join the university and was admitted to the Physical Science Stream in September 1970. The next year I joined the Engineering Faculty. But, after finishing the first semester courses, due to students' riot, all second year students at the Engineering Faculty were suspended for one year and had to start the next year in the second semester. After waiting idly for one year, again I started the engineering courses in the second semester. This time I was very frustrated that I couldn't score well, especially in Engineering Mathematics I got "F".

In 1974, the conditions in Ethiopia did not allow me to continue my university education, so like every Eritrean I decided to join the Eritrean Armed Struggle for Liberation at the end of 1974 and the dream of finishing university vanished. In the field, after completing political and military training I was assigned to a military hospital. After one year service in the hospital I was assigned to one of the fighting battalions as a barefoot doctor. In the beginning of the year 1978 I was wounded severely at my right leg that took six months to be cured in the hospital. After that I couldn't serve in the fighting army anymore because the wound has resulted in a foot-drop problem and I can't run or jump any more. At present, it has improved a lot that no one can notice it.

In June 1978 I was assigned to the Revolution School as a teacher, since I was not fit for the fighting army anymore. Then, after teaching for two years, I was sent to Sudan to teach Eritrean refugee children. There, I served both as a teacher, school director, coordinator of schools as well as in political mobilisation and organisation until independence.

After Independence, I was assigned at the curriculum development division as head of the science panel. In 1993, I became the coordinator of the mother tongue as well as the head of the Tigrigna mother tongue curriculum development. In August 1994 I was sent to the UK for an advanced post-graduate diploma at the University of Leeds for one year. After completing my post-graduate education, I came back home in August 1995.

At the beginning of 1996 I was assigned as coordinator of the secondary curriculum development division and served until 2003. During my service as the head of the secondary curriculum unit, I had a lot of responsibilities such as conducting curriculum surveys, conducting different workshops, such as curriculum orientation to new teachers be they nationals or expatriates, coordinating curriculum core teams to work in cooperation with the different subject panels in the development of curriculum, developing textbook writers from school teachers, conducting consultation workshops of newly developed textbooks in order to get a feedback from teachers before it was ready for printing, conducting competence tests at different levels to see the basic performance and disparity among our students at national level.

I have also been a member of many task forces. For example, a task force which was assigned to prepare a general methodology manual in science education for elementary and junior level. I have been a chairperson of the working group formed by MoE in cooperation with the University of Asmara to assess our current situation and formulate recommendations aimed at improving practical teaching in Eritrean high schools. I have served as a member of the supervising committee for the Review of

ESECE answer sheets formed by the University of Asmara to see answer sheets of some appealing students from 1998 – 2002. Now I am still a member of the task force for reviewing some appealing students in the General Examination of 8th Grade. I have also been a member of the task force that has been sponsored by the Ministry of Health in cooperation with MoE to organise and conduct a Drama Contest among high schools pertaining a message of misconception about the etiology and improper modes of treatment of sexually transmitted diseases vis-à-vis the rational treatment on HIV-AIDS. I was also a member of the task force for organising Students' Cultural and Sports Festival 2000. I served as a member of the task force for the "Rapid Education Needs Assessment Study" organised by MoE in collaboration with UNICEF in June 2000 in the two war-affected regions of Gash Barka and Debub due to the border conflict war conducted for two years when about 1.5 million people of Eritrea became internally displaced victims. The minister has assigned me for a special task, i.e. to prepare citizenship education syllabus for the three levels: elementary, junior and secondary. Now, textbooks are under preparation. Beyond all that I participated in several workshops of continuing training and national and international conferences.

IV. Raised in Times of War – Eritrea's Younger Generation

A Postwar Career

By Daniel Gebrehiwet Mengstab

After I accomplished my secondary and technical school education in 2001 from Wina technical school, I got a passing result in the Eritrean Secondary School Leaving Certificate Examination (ESSLCE). I joined the University of Asmara for diploma programme as regular student. I studied in the Department of Geography education for two years. At this time I have taken some courses of geography and education which enabled me to become geography teacher; the emphasis of my studies was to understand the fundamental geographical concepts and educational principles that govern modern development, but I also learned about other diverse topics such as research methodology, curriculum development and history. I found the topics on education (curriculum) to be very interesting and exciting; when I see it in the perspective my present career aspirations are to advance the curriculum development and planning in technical and vocational education in Eritrea.

Following the completion my diploma education in 2003, I got enough cumulative G.P.A (minimum 2.5 required, but I had 2.65) to advance to the degree programme. When we were learning in the diploma programme almost half of the courses were taken with degree programme, as a result the university legally exempted those courses for already taken in the diploma programme. In addition to this, those courses were also evaluated and credited with those degree programme students. Since then I joined the degree programme for three years (2003 to 2006) in the Department of Geography, which I have taken all the necessary geography and educational courses requirements and awarded B.A degree enables me to join master's programme at any time and university.

As a result of completing my university education I started to teach in Maihabar Technical School for one year. At that time I used to teach wood work and geography, as well as I have been working as a chairman of committee and coordinator of youth festival in the school. Then I was transferred to the National Centre for Vocational Training. Meanwhile I was doing my national and university service; in this place I have been working as the head of department and coordinator of the school. At that time the Centre was at the establishment stage and I am one the founders of the Centre. My main role was the allocation of teachers, leading departments, as well as the material and pedagogic control of the school. In addition I was advising new teachers so that they were able to develop their pedagogical and subject matter potentials. I have been working in such activities for one year of establishment. Then I became pedagogic head in the centre for about two and half years. In addition to the routine activities like teachers allocation, time table drafting, intramural supervision, I was coordinating the preparation of complied notes used as text book until text book becomes published. Those complied notes were really the foundation for the establishment of those text books. Meanwhile I used to provide pedagogical trainings for the teachers in the centre and its surrounding.

As mentioned above before I joined the University in 2001, I studied in Wina technical school and graduated in wood work technology. After accomplishing my technical education I used to work in several companies. Even after joining the University of Asmara, I used to work in some workshops during vacation. When working, it was clear to me that what we learned in the technical school cannot fit with what we got in the companies or industries. This is not only my personal experience, but also many of my class mates and later my students had similar feelings after joining the world of work. As a result they started to learn new skills which were totally different from what they already acquired in the technical school. Some of them even left the job in search of convenient work. Based on these facts I always dreamed of changing the curriculum. I got an opportunity in the university to take some education courses, with background of technical and vocational education and I had also taken some courses of curriculum development at the University of Asmara while I was doing my B.A degree which I consider as a blessing to realize my dream.

Currently the dream seems to be realised because I am working in the curriculum division of Technical and Vocational Education and Training (TVET). I was always eager to participate in the development of the competency based curriculum. Formerly our Eritrean technical vocational education curriculum development was directly copied (adopted) from outside, which could not fit for the Eritrean industries which are the main labour market of the graduated students. It really was a great loss for a poor nation like Eritrea, investing a huge amount of capital for such incomplete technical and vocational education. With further development of the Eritrean educational system the ground becomes comfortable for amendment of the former curriculum. Currently in most developed countries the common practice of developing technical education curriculum is the competency based curriculum. The graduates should be able to practice what they learned in relation to what the industries expect from them. Industries should participate in the development of the curriculum.

As an example one method that is especially important and that has been used repeatedly around the world for years especially in order to investigate vocational qualification is the DACUM method, an acronym for Developing A CurriculUM which I suggest the curriculum of Eritrean technical and vocational education should relay on.

"DACUM as used widely today is unique, innovative methods of job and/or occupational analysis, it is also very effective for conducting process and functional analysis. The DACUM analysis workshop involves trained DACUM facilitators and a committee of work expert workers from the position, occupational, or other areas of analysis" (Lipsmeier 2010, p.33).

To further development of my career aspirations as part of curriculum development team, I want to obtain a Master's Degree in curriculum studies. Having this knowledge will allow me to better understand educational principles especially in curriculum development. With all the uncertainty and changes in the world, politically, economically and technologically, I believe that education must have a solid understanding, supported by a strong academic foundation, of how to draft the curriculum through these challenging times.

No education is complete without experience. Armed with a solid understanding of academic principles, I can enhance my career. My experience I will add. Because I will be well versed in the theory, I will be able to adapt and modify the theoretical constructs as required in order to meet my country's needs. I fully recognise that our political, economic and technological environment is constantly changing and the curriculum needs to be able to adapt quickly and accurately to the new conditions if the country is to survive, let alone prosper. I believe obtaining a Master's Degree will provide the necessary background for me to anticipate and react to ever-changing environments and technologies. I look forward to launching my career.

To day I am working at the Ministry of Education, TVET department division of curriculum and planning. I joined this department because I have both technical and educational background. I have also been working in the national centre for vocational training as pedagogic head in the management staff. Currently we are working on the competency based curriculum development of technical and vocational education. Competency based education means that students should be able to practically apply what they know. This means students should develop the cognitive domain as well, as psychomotor and affective domains.

Competency is the ability to perform activities within an occupation at standards expected of an employee. This makes TVET much more relevant to meet the needs of industry and user agencies.

The crucial element of competency-based training programmes is to develop a curriculum based on occupational standards in each level of training and to assess the competencies required in each level. Generally, our activity in the process of curriculum planning and development is identification of training needs, evaluation of the existing programme, designing an improved programme and implement a new programme and then back to evaluating.

In addition we also collect labour market information and analyse it in-depth. Occupational analysis is used as a base. The activities involve inviting specific field or trade experts from industry and teachers/instructors. The major jump in this curriculum development in technical and vocational education is that the courses become modular in form. Modules are units of learning or sections of work organised with particular structural characteristics. Modules are an instructional package that includes a planned series of learning experiences designed to help the student mastering learning objectives. They are described as units of work, which are short, clear-cut and very specific in their purpose and evaluation is needed.

The modularisation of TVET programmes involves breaking up longer courses into shorter programmes. Each of these programmes is capable of being assessed as each element or subject. Each module extends from the beginning to the end of a semester and runs independently; two or more modules can go parallel from the beginning to the end of a semester and may consist of two or more chapters or units.

This all belongs to the team I am currently working in. Although the team involves all trades, I mainly focus on wood work and carpentry curriculum development and planning.

Experience and the Will to Improve

By Nur Ahmed Idris

Education or learning of any type generally brings about some kind of personal social professional and development changes in the individual. This particular Master programme has really brought a lot of change in my daily activity as a personality and a professional practitioner. Personally, I have acquired and developed the skill of putting activities into programme. After reading all the modules, I have come to clearly understand that planning is one aspect and fundamental perquisite to achievement in daily life.

In my work place, though I had a good knowledge of planning I used to do it single-handed as boss. I had very little skill in involving others to share competences in making a plan. Before this programme, I was not that good at communicating with the colleagues working with me or those who are under my management. But eventually I believe I've acquired fairly good listening skills. Now I think, I'm good at listening to others and they make their point heard.

Another important concept which I am still trying to integrate into my daily school practice is the personal reflection. Previously, I used to conduct various assessment practices in the form of meeting, seminars and workshops just to evaluate work progress. However, getting into this master's education programme has made me realize that assessment is not only checking work progress as such, but something that goes to the very depth of one's own personal reflection on a daily basis. Personal clarity and continuous inventory of the self is the best practice I've learned from the programme.

In fact my understanding of the system of school development was quite limited, but now I have got the full picture of what school quality is in terms of its organisational, personal and teaching aspects.

Last, but not least, handling educational problems and challenges in our work environment is what I have developed by now. The research methodologies I've studied and the reflection portfolio and seminar papers I've tried so far have helped me to develop a clear understanding of how to solve a specific educational challenge with a systematic empirical approach.

Generally, I've really acquired much knowledge and skills of school development and the above mentioned are some among many. Therefore I can definitely witness that this overall programme has supported me to have a wide perspective of systemic management of the school, if quality is to be achieved in our education system.

My general work experience is mainly related to education sector and the competencies I obtained in my long working experience are about the education system. The competence I developed during the past 20 years in the Ministry of Education is something that includes good leadership, common sense, conflict management, collaborative work and the will to learn from the experience of others.

Eritrea got independent in 1993. Once Eritrea got independent, the main goal was to meet the requirements of institutional working conditions and to develop competences to provide efficient and effective service in all sectors. In my experience, as an ex-fighter, it was challenging for me to assess and develop competences in the given institutions (Ministry of Education), because I had no training or orientation in the process of becoming a teacher.

At first I was assigned as teacher in Badda in 1992. Since then, as the result of my accumulated work experience and competences, I was assigned as subject teacher and coordinator of two schools. I have delivered some of the important contributions towards the work place such as writing instructional materials in my mother tongue, namely the Afar language.

I was assigned as school director in Eddi, a school found in southern red sea sub region of central Dankalia, where I developed a programme to solve managing conflicts (creating good relationship with staff, work collaboratively). It was very supportive and helpful to develop my competences towards professional development at that place. It was a big jump for me for my further professional development.

Unfortunately since 1998 I have been assigned as head of a Sub-Regional educational office. The skills and competences I developed were even more creditable and applicable at this place. I became more familiar with instructional materials, learning needs assessment, school policy and concept documents of the MoE. I also made situation analysis of curriculum developing strategy, coordinated and evaluated the school programme, created a suitable atmosphere for teacher performance improvement and also ensured effective learning regarding academic achievement and holistic development. Working intensively for 6 years I could confidently learn a lot which helped me to contribute something at my work place.

In 1996 I got a chance to join an in-service training programme as Educational Administrator at Bristol University. This helped me to reflect on my experience and development of competences at my work place. It enhanced my understanding of educational planning and management in specific areas.

My competence development towards education grew at a high rate of speed, because the ministry gave me a lot of opportunities to build my capacity. As the member of the organisation I was able to develop such important competences as to act efficiently and competently. I can say all these served as the foundation to my current competence.

In 2001 the Ministry of Education started to expand management skills in the line of organisation at national level. I got a chance to go abroad for an advanced diploma in education for two years. I got professional input to develop my efficiency towards the work ground. The emphasis of the course was on formal education. This helped me to promote my competences through critical self- reflection. After finishing I came back to my country and was assigned for new job as the head of adult education and media at the regional level. This new position has improved my ability and learning skills. I organised a mobilisation programme in different areas of the region. This was to build up effectiveness in work performance in the teaching and learning processes.

After the long way through the process of gradually changing my professional development and educational upgrading, my current position is acting as the head of basic education at regional level. I was appointed to this job in 2008. I'd like to emphasise the need to sustain, enhance and upgrade my current competence along the lines of my expected role and responsibilities. I got a chance for a 2 years course in Denmark. This was really an encouraging and enlightening occasion and a turning point for me to acquire a sound educational base.

I was in a good position, ready to acquire good knowledge of the broad areas of the educational system in general and how to apply it to the specific purpose of "Basic Education". What is important here is that my long experience and training helped me in a position to be confident.

Glossary

Barefoot Doctor: A community health worker (a community consists of about 1,000 to 1,500 households, there could be up to three villages in one community). He is only allowed to prescribe limited drugs and he is trained for a very short period of about six months. He is at the lowest hierarchy level of the medical staff. In many cases a barefoot doctor is the first contact to normal households in need of health services.

Eritrean Liberation Front (ELF): After the neutralization of the Eritrean Liberation Movement (ELM) a new organization of Eritrean nationalists named ELF was formed by Eritrean expatriates in Cairo in 1960. In contrast to the ELM the ELF was bent on waging armed struggle on behalf of Eritrean independence from the outset. The ELF was composed mainly of Eritrean Muslims from the rural lowlands on the western edge of the territory. In 1961 the ELF's political character was vague, but radical Arab states such as Syria and Iraq sympathized with Eritrea as a predominantly Muslim region struggling to escape oppression and imperial domination. These two countries therefore supplied military and financial assistance to the ELF. The ELF initiated military operations in 1961 and intensified its activities in response to the dissolution of the federation in 1962. By 1967 the ELF had gained considerable support among peasants, particularly in Eritrea's north and west and around the port city of Massawa. Haile Selassie attempted to calm the growing unrest by visiting Eritrea and by assuring its inhabitants that they would be treated as equals under the new arrangements. Although he doled out offices, money and titles in early 1967, in the hope he could co-opting would-be Eritrean opponents, the resistance persisted.

By 1971 the activity of the ELF had become such a serious threat that the emperor declared martial law in Eritrea and deployed roughly half his army to contain the struggle at the same time. Internal disputes over strategy and tactics, however, eventually led to the ELF's fragmentation and the founding of another group in 1972: the Eritrean People's Liberation Front (EPLF).

Source: Library of Congress – Federal Research Division Country Profile: Eritrea, September 2005; this article is available under:

http://lcweb2.loc.gov/frd/cs/profiles/Eritrea.pdf

Eritrean Liberation Movement (ELM): ELM which began its activities in 1958 was a militant opposition to the incorporation of Eritrea into Ethiopia. It was as an organization made up mainly by students, intellectuals and urban wage laborers. The ELM engaged in clandestine political activities and intended to cultivate resistance to the centralizing policies of the imperial state. By 1962, however, the ELM had been discovered and destroyed by imperial authorities.

Source: Library of Congress – Federal Research Division Country Profile: Eritrea, September 2005; this article is available under:

http://lcweb2.loc.gov/frd/cs/profiles/Eritrea.pdf

Eritrean People's Liberation Front (EPLF): Internal disputes over strategy and tactics eventually led to the ELF's fragmentation and the founding of another group, the EPLF in 1972. The leadership of this multiethnic movement came to be dominated by leftist and Christian dissidents who spoke Tigrinya, Eritrea's predominant language. Sporadic armed conflict ensued between the two groups from 1972 to 1974, even as they fought Ethiopian forces.

In September 1974 a group of Ethiopian military officers deposed the emperor and established a military government in Addis Ababa known as the Derg, which allied itself with the

Soviet Union. The Derg immediately turned its attention to the Eritrean question. Some in its ranks pressed for a decisive military solution, while others favored a negotiated settlement. Influential Derg nationalists, like its predecessors –the imperial regime-, endorsed the ideal of "Greater Ethiopia"; that is a unitary, multiethnic state and eventually decided to continue to use force in dealing with Eritrean secessionists. In response, the ELF and EPLF maintained their struggle for Eritrean independence. Armed conflict between the Derg and (mostly) the EPLF continued throughout the 1970s and 1980s, with neither side able to score a decisive victory. In particular, the EPLF stronghold at Nakfa in northern Eritrea withstood repeated assaults by the Ethiopian army. Beginning in March 1988, a series of offensives against demoralized Ethiopian forces eventually led the EPLF to control entire Eritrea by late May 1991. At the same time when the EPLF was defeating the Ethiopian army in Eritrea, Tigrayan and allied rebel forces took over northern Ethiopia and drove the Derg from power. Following a UN supervised referendum, nearly 100 percent of Eritreans favoured separation. Eritrea gained independence from Ethiopia on May 24, 1993 - a development many Ethiopians opposed. Isaias Afwerki, the leader of the EPLF, became the first president of Eritrea. In 1994 the EPLF became a political party - the People's Front for Democracy and Justice.

Source: Library of Congress – Federal Research Division Country Profile: Eritrea, September 2005; this article is available under:

http://lcweb2.loc.gov/frd/cs/profiles/Eritrea.pdf

Revolution Schools: In addition to the Zero School, the EPLF started to establish and to maintain regular schools in the liberated, predominantly rural areas. Schools had often to be camouflaged against air attacks and students had to be prepared to take cover. The numbers of the Revolution Schools vary with the area and people in the liberated zones. In 1990 there were 165 schools administered by the EPLF, with 1782 teachers serving about 27 000 students.

Zero School: In the mid-1970s the liberated areas under the control of the EPLF began to expand and ushering the beginnings of a national school system the EPLF established a kind of pilot school named "Zero School" in the north of Eritrea in 1976. The school was designed as a boarding school for orphans, refugees, children of fighters and those who had run away to join the front but were too young to fight. The Zero School started with about 150 students and a handful of teachers. It can be seen as a teaching laboratory and a workshop for the expanding education system. The Zero School eventually offered five years of elementary education and two years of middle school, adding grades as students continued climbing the education ladder. By 1983, the school had more than 3,000 students. A national adult literacy campaign was startet at the same time with the dispatch of 451 teenage Zero School students to serve as teachers behind enemy lines.

Zoba: The term "Zoba" designates an administrative district. Eritrea has six zobas which are further split into sub-zobas.

About the Authors

Abraham Russom Almedom

Born 1954 in Dekidashim, Eritrea Abraham Russom Almedom studied until the mid of second year at Addis Ababa University in the faculty of science. Then he withdrew to join the Eritrean Peoples' Liberation Front (EPLF). in 1975. Already during his soldier time he was a teacher and one of the coordinators of literacy programme aiming at EPLF members as well as people from the liberated areas. Later on he was assigned as a teacher, curriculum developer and school manager in a revolution school. Before and after independence he participated in various short term professional training courses, including a one year course at UNESCO IIEP (International institute for educational planning) in Paris. He also worked in different positions in the educational sector and today he is the director of curriculum planning and development of general education in the Ministry of Education.

Daniel Ghebrehiwet Mengstab

Born 1983 in Dengel, Eritrea Daniel Ghebrehiwet Mengstab accomplished his secondary and technical school in 2001. In 2006 he obtained a Bachelor of Arts degree in Geography from the University of Asmara and started to teach in Maihabr technical school as a teacher of geography and wood working. In 2008 he moved to the national center for vocational training where he had different positions. In 2010 he became a team member of the curriculum development and planning division in the Ministry of Education head department of TVET.

Ghebrezghi Dimam Okbaldet

Ghebrezghi Dimam Okbaldet was born 1947 in Dorok, Eritrea. After finishing senior secondary education in 1969 he joined the college of teacher education in Addis Ababa. In 1974 he started teaching in a junior school in eastern Ethiopia. In 1981 he joined the Eritrean liberation struggle and was placed to "Zero School" where he became a member of the curriculum team and later on a senior supervisor. After Eritrea's independence he served in several positions within the educational sector and today he is the director general of the adult & media education department in the Ministry of Education.

Ghirmai Estifanos Tesfu

Born 1952 in Keren, Eritrea Ghirmai Estifanos Tesfu graduated in metal technology at the polytechnic institute in Ethiopia. 1977 he joined the Eritrean Peoples' Liberation Front and became next to his soldier life a teacher of vocational education and training in the liberated areas. After independence he continued to work in the educational sector and today he is the director for curriculum planning and development in the TVET department of the Ministry of Education. 2002 he obtained a bachelor degree in education from the University of Huddersfield, United Kingdom.

Girmai Gebrehiwet Azbeha

Born 1952 in Nefasit in the region of northern red sea Girmai Gebrehiwet Azbeha entered the teacher training institute in Addis Ababa in 1972/73. After serving two years as an elementary school teacher in the southern part of Ethiopia, he joined the Eritrean armed struggle in 1975. After being wounded he was assigned as a teacher in a boarding school which gathered children of nomads, fighters and from displaced people. Later he worked 8 years as a school director of an Eritrean refugee school in Sudan. After independence he worked in several positions for the MoE and obtained in 1999 a certificate in educational planning and administration from IIEP, Paris. Currently he is the head of zoba Maekel education office in the ministry of education.

Hailu Asfaha Foto

Due to the Eritrean-Ethiopian war Hailu Asfaha Foto, born in 1956 in Mai-Habar, Eritrea left his studies at Addis Ababa University and joined the Eritrean armed struggle in 1975. After being wounded he was assigned to be teacher in the Eritrean Peoples' Liberation Front department of education in the liberated areas. He worked as a teacher and later principal in the revolution schools inside Eritrea as well as in schools built for Eritrean refugees in Sudan. After independence he had been working in various areas of the educational sector; in 1997 he obtained an international diploma in educational planning and administration from NIEPA, India; 2001 he obtained an international diploma in educational planning and management from IIEP, Paris and currently he is the director of research and statistics division in the ministry of education.

Kaleab Andemichael Bairue

Born 1954 in Adi-Chindog, Eritrea Kaleab Andemichael Bairue graduated from the teacher training institute in 1966 and underwent different stations as a teacher. In 1987 he obtained a Diploma in mathematics from the Bahridar Teacher's College. In 2003 he obtained a Bachelor of Science degree in mathematics from the University of Asmara and currently he is a mathematics curriculum developer in the Department of General Education Curriculum division in the Ministry of Education.

Mehreteab Dirar Gebresilassie

Born in 1940 at Firdgi, Eritrea Mehreteab Dirar Gebresilassie obtained a Bachelor of Arts degree in history and minor in geography at Addis Ababa University in 1990. Since 1963 he was working as a teacher at different levels (from elementary up to secondary schools). At present since 2007, he is a curriculum developer in the Department of General Education in the Ministry of Education.

Nur Ahmed Idris

Born 1972 in Massawa, Eritrea Nur Ahmed Idris joined at the age of 14 the armed struggle, where he first became a student and later a fighter. After the end of the war he was assigned as an elementary school teacher and coordinator of two schools in the Northern Red Sea Region. In the following years he went through several positions in the educational sector and now he is the head of basic education for the Southern Red Sea Region in the Ministry of Education.

Petros Hailemariam

Born in 1950 in Dekemhare, Eritrea. Petros Hailemariam withdrew from his science studies at Addis Ababa University to join the Eritrean People's Liberation Front. In 1975 he was one of the persons assigned to set up a department of education within the EPLF and the first EPLF- run school in the field, of which he became a director later on. After independence he served in several positions within the educational sector and today he is the director general of the research and human resource department in the ministry of education.

Tesfalidet Tecle Ghebremariam

Born 1958 in Asmara, Eritrea Tesfalidet Tecle Ghebremariam suffered like a lot of his generation of the conflict between Eritrea and Ethiopia as he could not continuously go to school. He joined like a lot of his friends the armed struggle in 1977 and was later on (1983) assigned as a teacher and school principal in elementary and boarding schools. Through a distance study programme he obtained a post graduate diploma in management from Leicester University, United Kingdom in 1998. Today he is the head of the supervision unit in the department of TVET in the Ministry of Education.

Tquabo Aimut Gebreselassie

Tquabo Aimut Gebreselassie was born in 1952 in Sarda, Eritrea. After finishing secondary school he joined the Eritrean Peoples' Liberation Front in 1975. He worked as an elementary school teacher in the liberated areas and as a school principal in an Eritrean refugee school in Sudan. After independence he continued to work in the educational sector and is nowadays the division head of the national curriculum planning and development for adult and non-formal education in the Ministry of Education. In 1997 he obtained diploma from the Institute of Adult Education in Tanzania and in 2001 an international diploma of the IIEP, Paris in educational planning and management.

Yosief Tewelde Negusse

Born 1951 in Harien, Eritrea Yosief Tewolde Negusse studied from 1971-1974 engineering at the Haile Selassie University in Addis Ababa and received an advanced diploma in educational science of the University of Leeds, United Kingdom in 1995. During the Eritrean struggle for liberation he joined the Eritrean Peoples' Liberation Front where he began to work as a barefoot doctor. After having been seriously wounded in the field he was assigned as a teacher in the revolution schools and also taught Eritrean refugee children in Sudan. After the independence of Eritrea in 1993 he was assigned for several tasks in the curriculum development division at the Ministry of Education where he is still working as a coordinator in the curriculum development department.

www.ingramcontent.com/pod-product-compliance
Lightning Source LLC
Chambersburg PA
CBHW050655270326
41927CB00012B/3039